# THE FALL OF AN EMPIRE

# THE FALL OF AN EMPIRE

## THE FINAL DAYS OF THE VIJAYANAGARA KINGDOM

ABHIJEETH HILIYANA

An imprint of
Srishti Publishers & Distributors

**Srishti Publishers & Distributors**
A unit of AJR Publishing LLP
212A, Peacock Lane
Shahpur Jat, New Delhi – 110 049

editorial@srishtipublishers.com

First published in India by Bold,
an imprint of Srishti Publishers & Distributors in 2024



10 9 8 7 6 5 4 3 2 1

This is a work of non-fiction, based on the author's thorough research and experience. While due care has been taken to verify all information at press time, any inadvertent miss brought to notice shall be updated in the subsequent editions.



Printed and bound in India

*To my wife Divya.*
*Without your encouragement,*
*this book would not have become a reality.*

# *Acknowledgments*

I would like to thank my wife Divya, whose constant encouragement helped me bring this novel to life.

My father and brother, for always supporting my writing.

I would also like to thank Suhail Mathur and the Book Bakers literary agency team for helping me bring this book to you through Srishti Publishers.

The team at Srishti, Stuti Gupta and Arup Bose, for patiently working on the book and seeing it through to completion.

I would also like to thank all my friends, who took the extra effort to listen to my story patiently and gave me valuable feedback.

# CHAPTER 1
# 1564

The day he had been dreading had finally arrived. To say he was surprised would have been a lie. Venkatadri had always suspected that all their actions over the past decades would lead to this very outcome. Worse, he knew that his brother Ramaraya was aware of it as well. *Yet you carried on, Anna. Knowing fully well the consequence,* he thought bitterly.

"What shall I tell Mahaprabhu?" the messenger asked warily.

Venkatadri had been woken up early in the morning by an urgent message from his brother, requesting his presence at the royal durbar.

"You can tell my brother that I will arrive on time," he said. The messenger bowed respectfully and walked back the way he had come. Venkatadri sat on his seat, deep in thought. The palace was an hour away; his brother preferred to hold it at the first hour after sunrise.

"Is there a point in my going?" he wondered. He knew the reason for the summons. A messenger from the Bijapur Sultan had arrived in the capital and had demanded a meeting with Ramaraya.

Demand it, did he? Venkatadri mused. Once again, he was not surprised. They had been hearing constant reports from their spies in the Shahi kingdoms for several months. All of them had been busy preparing their armies. Hussain Nizam Shah had even recruited nearly ten thousand mercenaries from Khorasan. A huge force, but even more astonishingly, had not caused much concern among his neighbours. It did not need a genius to figure out what the Shahis were planning. Indeed, it was quite simple as just a few months back, the sultanates had strengthened their alliances through marriages. Hussain Shah's two daughters were married to Ali Adil Shah and Ibrahim Qutb Shah, and Ali Adil Shah's sister was married to Murtaza Nizam Shah, the son of Hussain Nizam Shah. There was only one target, Samrajya.

"It was long overdue," he sighed. He stood up, clasping his hands behind his back, his eyes closed as he tried to control his rising anger. He had warned his brother time and again, but each time Ramaraya had ignored his concerns.

"They are mere children; how can they harm us?" his brother had laughed. The words still echoed in Venkatadri's mind. His brother's arrogance had angered Venkatadri. That and the casual regard he appeared to possess for the people of Samrajya. Except, Venkatadri had understood that there was more to his brother's reaction than simple arrogance.

"He wants this battle, as badly as they," Venkatadri growled. He heard the sharp intake of breath of his two guards, but Venkatadri's fierce glare caused them to look down at the ground. Venkatadri went back to his thoughts where he only found anger at his brother's actions and ambitions.

From the day Ramaraya had been appointed as the guardian of the young emperor, he had worked towards a single goal – to replace the Tuluva dynasty with their own family, the Aravidu. Except he had gone about achieving it in the most indirect manner.

"He should have done what Saluva Narasimha did or what Vira Narasimha, emperor Krishnadevaraya's elder brother had done and overthrown the emperor."

It might have led to a period of instability and rebellions, but Venkatadri was confident that ultimately, they would have brought the empire under their rule successfully. It would have been simple and decisive. But their brother had not done that. Instead, over the three decades after he had gained power, he had slowly and steadily usurped the power of the emperor, reducing him to a mere figurehead. Everyone had expected Ramaraya to crown himself as the new emperor afterwards, but Ramaraya had not replaced him, instead continuing with the perverse arrangement. Venkatadri had been left wondering about the reason behind his brother's strange reluctance. Was it lack of confidence that his action would be accepted by the common populace or was it vestigial loyalty towards the memory of his father-in-law Krishnadevaraya? Venkatadri was not certain.

"Prabhu, shall I ask the stable master to prepare your horse for the ride to the palace compound?" asked his bodyguard. Venkatadri shook his head.

"There is still time. I will walk," he said.

"But Prabhu..." the guard protested as if surprised at Venkatadri's strange decision.

"This is my city as well, Byrappa. I will be safe," he smiled. Byrappa bowed.

Venkatadri changed into a simple white *antariya* and silk shirt. He wore no decorations save for his purple *kulavi,* which was studded with rubies and diamonds, indicating his position as the commander in chief of the Samrajya armies. He ran his hand over his head, noting the greying hair. His face was clean-shaven but for a small moustache. He liked keeping it small even though he knew a great many commanders considered having a luxuriant moustache the mark of a true nobleman. He wondered how the fad had started. Now everyone, including his two brothers and almost all his nephews, possessed large moustaches. Even his sons possessed them.

If only our enemies ran at the sight of our fearsome moustaches, Venkatadri thought tiredly. He forced his mind away from the negative thoughts. He examined himself in the mirror once more, making sure he was ready for the durbar. At sixty-one, Venkatadri was past his prime. But he had still managed to retain a great amount of his youthful strength through daily strenuous exercises. But the signs of his age were still quite evident.

How much longer will I be able to continue? He wondered. His brother was strong, despite being eighty years old. As was his other brother Tirumala at seventy-two. In comparison to both, Venkatadri was still 'young'. But will it be enough? he wondered as he walked outside to his waiting guards.

"The meeting will be in an hour, and I do not wish to hurry, so we will leave now," he declared.

Byrappa nodded and directed the soldiers to assume position around Venkatadri. With a final sigh, Venkatadri stepped into the streets and walked towards the royal compound.

***

Venkatadri could see that almost everyone who stood in the hall that day was in favour of the war. The hunger in their eyes evident, yet they continued the farce of negotiation. The Bijapur envoy was a young man, barely in his twenties. His manner was impervious as he recounted the instances when Samrajya had failed to consider Bijapur's grievances and the times that Samrajya took advantage of Bijapur's weakness to capture its territory. No more, he cried, Sultan Ali Adil Shah had finally decided that it was enough. But as a peace-loving man, the Sultan was willing to give Samrajya one more chance but on the condition that Vijayanagara handed over the region around Raichur Doab along with the fortress of Raichur as tribute. On failing to do so, the Sultan would personally lead his armies to show Vijayanagara the true power of Bijapur.

Venkatadri watched his older brother, take in the speech with great equanimity. Once it was done, he extended his left hand to the side and his betel leaf bearer handed him a *thambula*. Ramaraya put it in his mouth continuing to chew slowly as if in deep thought.

"What is your answer?" the envoy demanded.

Ramaraya smiled, his lips red due to the thambula.

"Did you just see me eat this thambula?" he asked.

The envoy was confused by the question.

"Prabhu?" he said, "I..."

"I asked if you saw me eating this thambula?"

"I did, Prabhu," the envoy nodded.

"Is it possible for me to give it back to my betel bearer if he wants it back?"

"No, that would be quite impossible," the envoy replied.

"Correct. Do you know why he gave me the thambula?"

"Because he is your servant?"

"That is true, but more importantly, because he is completely dependent on me, both for his livelihood and protection. Your Sultan has a rather short memory, but I am sure he would remember that it was I who saved him and his kingdom when he was under attack by Ibrahim Qutb Shah and Hussain Nizam Shah just a few years ago. If I had failed to aid him on that day, then Bijapur would have been destroyed. You can also remind him that he and his kingdom have lived in peace and prosperity after that incident because his enemies were afraid to provoke the mighty armies of Samrajya as your Sultan was under my protection. Raichur was a thambula, an offering that your sultan made to obtain Samrajya's aid. Samrajya has already accepted that offering and the fort and its surrounding areas are now a part of the empire. How can we return it? Just as I cannot return the thambula in my stomach, so too Samrajya cannot return Raichur."

"There is a difference between a piece of land and food, Prabhu," the envoy said stiffly.

"Is it? Just as we consume food for sustenance, kingdoms need to consume land to grow and prosper. Is that not the same reason that your Sultan is eyeing Raichur?"

"He is not eyeing anything that does not belong to him. Raichur has always been part of Bijapur," the envoy argued.

"Yet Bijapur is less than a half century old. What about before that?" Tirumala Raya asked suddenly. He was literally shaking with excitement. Unlike Venkatadri, his brother Tirumala had always been more of an administrator than a soldier and it was reflected in his physique. He was lean, a great deal thinner than Venkatadri and thinner than Ramaraya in his prime. He had delicate hands; his face looked considerable younger than he was. In fact, many people thought Venkatadri was older to him than the other way around. It was Tirumala who had streamlined the administration after Ramaraya assumed power. He was the prime minister in all but name. But he desired more, while he was widely respected for his skills as administrator, Tirumala felt he never received the same praise for his soldierly skills compared to his brothers. For Tirumala, it was one honour that he yearned for throughout his life and one that he felt had been forever denied.

"I have never had the opportunities to excel as you did, brother," Tirumala had told Venkatadri often when the two of them had been inspecting the army regiments.

Venkatadri did not know how to respond to that statement. He had fought in multiple battles and with each passing battle, he had lost his desire for more, despairing the constant bloodshed. The veteran in him hesitated, but he understood that for a soldier, who had never experienced it, war was something that they had read about in poems and listened to in ballads. A glorious and noble venture which every true warrior must be excited to take part in.

So, it did not surprise him to see the hunger for glory in the eyes of many in the hall that day, including Tirumala. Yet Venkatadri felt that at least Ramaraya should hesitate. He had seen enough bloodshed to last a lifetime and was sure that he would not wish for more. But instead, his brother appeared to be happy to go into another war.

"Prabhu, before Bijapur, Raichur was part of Bahamani empire whose successor is our great nation," the envoy declared.

"And before the Bahamani empire?" asked the young man to Tirumala's right – his eldest son, Raghunatha who looked like a younger version of Tirumala. Behind him were his brothers, Sriranga and Venkata, who too looked eager. Venkatadri looked around the hall, recognising every assembled face. It was not difficult. Save for a few, most of them were his relatives. Cousins, nephews, and uncles were all there. Ramaraya had made sure that his kinsmen occupied the important positions in the empire, ensuring their loyalty.

A mistake, Venkatadri sighed. What they gained in loyalty, they lost in competence and in the coming struggle, loyalty would be useless.

"Prabhu, does it matter? By that logic, you will find that Raichur does not belong to Samrajya as well as the empire is only two centuries old," the envoy argued.

"Correct," Ramaraya smiled. "Then what decides ownership?" he asked.

“I am willing to hear your position, Prabhu,” the envoy replied.

“Possession. We hold Raichur and that makes it ours.”

“Is that your final answer?” the envoy asked.

“Yes,” Ramaraya said.

“Very well, I will take your response to my master. However, I fear he will not take kindly to this effort.”

“I will wait for him,” Ramaraya said unconcerned. The envoy turned and left the hall. Venkatadri noted pleasure in the man’s eyes.

Looks like everyone gets their wish; all except for me, he thought bitterly.

******

“Tirumala, I want you and your son to concentrate your forces on the southern bank of the Krishna River. How much time will it take you for full mobilisation?” Ramaraya demanded once the envoy had left the hall.

Tirumala glanced at his eldest son for an answer. “One week. We will be ready to march in a week,” Raghunatha said confidently.

Ramaraya seemed satisfied, “Good, and I want the rest of the assembled Nayakas to concentrate their armies at the capital. We must be ready to march at the earliest.”

“We will show these dogs the true power of Samrajya,” cried Sriranga.

“Yes, it is time we settle this once and for all,” Ramaraya agreed. “This meeting is over,” he declared.

Venkatadri stood where he was as he watched the room empty of people. Once the last man stood up, Ramaraya stood up and got down from his elevated perch.

“Walk with me, brother,” he said calmly as if aware that Venkatadri wished to speak to him privately. Venkatadri indicated to his own men to remain, and he walked with his brother. Ramaraya was silent the whole way, as he led Venkatadri to the royal gardens inside the compound which had been created during the time of the great Krishnadevaraya and expanded by Ramaraya.

"Do you know that when father-in-law had expressed his desire to create this garden inside the compound, his ministers tried to dissuade him as they felt it was a waste of water, especially since the city was still suffering from water shortage during the summer months. Do you know what he did?"

"He hired Portuguese engineers who improved the water situation of the city enormously."

"Yes, and he managed to solve a problem that had been plaguing Vijayanagara from decades. It was typical of him. There was not a single problem that he could not overcome if he put his mind to it. That is why he is worshipped by people even today. He gave us the confidence that if we put our mind to it, then Samrajya could achieve anything."

"Anna..." Venkatadri tried.

"What have I achieved?"

"You have expanded the empire further than even the great Krishnadevaraya. You have kept our country safe and prosperous."

"I have, haven't I? But still, I am not the emperor. I am simply a minister to a boy unqualified to rule this land."

Not that we gave him an opportunity to prove himself, Venkatadri thought annoyed, but he did not voice it out aloud. "Then why don't you assume the true power?"

Ramaraya turned to face him, a weary look on his face, "You think it is that easy, my brother? What do you think will the people say if I capture power now? That I have overthrown the rightful king."

"But that is how Saluva and Tuluva families came to power before you," Venkatadri argued.

"When Saluva Narasimha launched his rebellion, the empire was on the verge of collapsing, the people desperate for a strong hand after decades of misgovernance. When Vira Narasimha took power, he had to face rebellions throughout the empire. A full decade was required to quell the rebelling Nayakas. The last one, Gangaraja, dying only during the rule of Krishnadevaraya. I do not wish to spend the rest of my limited time in this world quelling rebellions."

"But Anna, there are hardly any powerful vassals left; we have replaced most of them with our own kinsmen. Surely, they will remain loyal."

"Maybe, but then there is the fact that I am seizing power from the family of Krishnadevaraya. How do you think the people will react?" he asked, an expression of pain clearly visible.

There it was! Venkatadri had finally understood the reason for his brother's reluctance. His brother was insecure, that despite all his achievements, he could never surpass his father-in-law, Krishnadevaraya.

"Anna, we face a formidable enemy army. Our spies have been sending regular reports of the large number of forces all the Sultans are recruiting. They have also been busy hiring thousands of mercenaries."

"It still won't be enough," Ramaraya said confidently.

"Anna, do not—"

"Venkatadri, there is no possible way we can avoid this battle without losing face. Do you think I should hand over the regions that they have demanded? What will be left of my authority if I did that? Worse, by surrendering those regions, I will open the empire's interior for enemy armies."

Venkatadri sighed deeply; his brother was right. It was too late. The sultanates would not agree for peace, not without complete humiliation of Vijayanagara and that would be unacceptable to any soldier of Vijayanagara. Still, they should have been careful in their previous dealings with the sultanates.

"The problem with wisdom is it usually comes too late," Ramaraya laughed as if guessing Venkatadri's thoughts.

"Anna, let me command the forces at Krishna," Venkatadri begged.

"No, we both know that you are the only capable commander that I have left since Keladi Sadashiva Nayaka is bedridden. He sent me a letter apologising for his failure to attend the annual Darbar." Venkatadri could see tears in his brother's eyes at the memory of his favourite commander.

"Will he recover?"

Ramaraya shook his head sadly, "No, which is why I need you here, to organise and prepare the main army for battle. Once that is done, we can lead it together."

"Anna, you don't need to concern yourself. Tirumala and I will be more than capable of winning this battle," Venkatadri replied horrified at the thought of his venerable brother marching to battle.

"You think I am too old to be on the battlefield?" Ramaraya demanded fiercely.

That is exactly what I think, Venkatadri thought but held his tongue.

Ramaraya grinned, "You were never reticent in expressing your opinions, my brother. What has happened?"

"What is the point of voicing them if no one will listen?" Venkatadri asked tiredly.

"I have always listened to them," Ramaraya said gently. "You have always been my voice of reason."

"Then I beg you to listen to me today. Let me command the armies at Krishna and let Tirumala lead the main army to my aid. You can remain here in the city. Your presence here will be a morale booster for the people."

"Krishnadevaraya would not have hidden behind his walls in case of a war," Ramaraya snapped.

"Krishnadevaraya is not eighty. Krishnadevaraya did not replace his officers with his kinsmen," Venkatadri growled.

Ramaraya shook his head, "You are right on both counts. I am too old to be walking, leave aside fighting on the battlefield," he grinned.

"Then let me do it. Have I ever failed you?" Venkatadri cried.

"No, but we both know this will be a great battle. On the same scale as the battle of Raichur, if not greater. As you have rightly observed, we lack capable officers, and you and Tirumala cannot be everywhere. I might be old, but I can still command an army. I will not stay behind inside the city."

"If you have already decided to ignore me, then why did you ask for my opinion?" Venkatadri demanded bitterly.

"Because this might be the only time, we might be able to speak freely before the battle," Ramaraya said softly.

Venkatadri hugged his aged brother tightly. He had been more like a father than a brother to him and Tirumala. Now this old man was determined to risk his life for his country and there was nothing that Venkatadri could do about it. Once more that day, Venkatadri felt deeply sad.

******

Ali Adil Shah wished for the fool to stop or at least focus on what was important. Like, planning the actual campaign for the coming war against Samrajya. But thinking was not Hussain Nizam Shah's strong suit; he was a warrior not a strategist. His skills lay in charging headfirst with his men and not worry about what was occurring around him. He had the build for it as well – a large man, well over six foot with the body of a wrestler. His face covered with a great mane of hair. He was dressed in chainmail as he graphically described what he would do to the enemy soldiers once he got his hands on them. In the corner was a small lean man, his head bent down, writing furiously. Aftabi was the favourite court poet of Nizam Shah, and it was his job to translate his master's crude ramblings into something more appropriate 'for the future generations' as Nizam Shah often declared. Nizam Shah cared a great deal about how he would be perceived in posterity, so he made great efforts to ensure that the 'right' version of history was recorded.

If he wastes another day with his rants, it would be Ramaraya who will be writing any future history and it would be over our dead bodies, Adil Shah thought wearily. And the old man could very well achieve it, of that Adil Shah had little doubt. Despite Hussain Nizam Shah's assertions of the vileness of Ramaraya, his treachery towards the sultanates and his supposed bloodthirstiness, Adil Shah knew that *they* were no different. Hussain Nizam Shah was angry that Ramaraya's forces had laid waste to his kingdom during the last war, but he seemed to have conveniently forgotten how Hussain Shah's father had done the same to the people of Bijapur during the reign of Ali's father. In fact, he had even invaded Ali's kingdom only a few years back with an intention of wiping out Bijapur Sultanate. It was Ramaraya who had come to his aid, saving his kingdom and people from certain destruction. That act of kindness had earned the old man a place in Ali's heart. Yet here he was, sitting with a man he hated, to wage a war against the man he loved. He would have laughed at the irony if he could, but Ali held his thoughts to himself.

Ruling a kingdom was truly a crown of thorns. Ali could love Ramaraya and call him father, but Ali Adil Shah could not ignore the fact that until Samrajya remained strong, Bijapur could never achieve its rightful position as the true inheritor of Bahamani Sultanate. For Bijapur to rise, Samrajya must be defeated. Ali knew that his kingdom could never do it on its own, so here he was, sharing a tent with the other sultanates, none for who he had any liking or kinship with. And he knew that the feeling was mutual.

All the sultanates had answered Nizam Shah's call that day. United for a single cause – the defeat of Samrajya. It was an alliance of convenience and if they achieved their objective, Ali was certain they would fall back to fight amongst themselves. Which was fine with him as Bijapur was still the most powerful of the sultanates.

He felt a hand on his shoulder which made him turn his head, "My Sultan, Sultan Nizam Shah asked you a question," Kishwar Khan said pleasantly. He was Ali's chief military commander, having served with Ali's father in multiple campaigns. He was in his late fifties with a thick grey beard and a gentle face. He was looking at Ali with some concern,

"Question?" Ali turned towards Hussain Nizam Shah who was scowling at him, annoyed at Ali's lack of attention.

"I asked the Sultan if he is willing to lend his support to our cause till the bitter end," he said with mock sweetness.

"Isn't that obvious! Why else do you think I am here with my forces," Ali almost blurted out but instead he forced a smile and declared loudly. "I will be honoured to be a part of this grand venture," bowing slightly in his seat.

Satisfied, Hussain Nizam Shah turned towards the next sultan, Ibrahim Qutb Shah who sat on Ali's left. Ibrahim Qutb Shah was the Sultan of Golconda, the second most powerful kingdom after Ali's own Bijapur. He was a lean man with the built of a cavalry archer with wide shoulders and powerful arms. His head was clean shaved with a felt silk cap, embroidered with golden threads, covering it completely.

"I do," Ibrahim Qutb Shah said instantly without waiting for Hussain Nizam Shah to ask the question. Ali knew the reason for the animosity the Ibrahim felt towards Ramaraya. Like Ali, Ibrahim owed his enthronement to Ramaraya. Ibrahim's brother, Jamsheed had ascended the throne by murdering their father and blinding their elder brother. Ibrahim had managed to save his life and find refuge with Ramaraya, and after the death of Jamsheed, Ibrahim gained the throne with help of Ramaraya. They maintained a friendly relationship for over a decade. Sadly, it was a friendship that was not destined to last. Ibrahim held genuine love and respect towards his patron. Unfortunately, Ramaraya, like Ali, cared only for Samrajya. When some of Ibrahim's disgruntled nobles revolted and invited Ramaraya to take control of important border forts, Ramaraya had jumped at the chance. Ibrahim managed to crush the rebellion before Samrajya armies arrived, but his belief in his friend and patron was shattered. Then Ramaraya had taken the side of Ali in the last war against Hussain Nizam Shah and Ibrahim Qutb Shah, which finally broke the last vestiges of affection that he held for Ramaraya. Now he was here to take revenge on the man who had betrayed him.

Hussain Nizam Shah smiled at Ibrahim, moving to the final ruler, Ali Barid Shah, the ruler of Bidar Sultanate, which was the smallest of the sultanates. Ali was not sure why the man was here, but he suspected it was less to do with the 'cause' and more to do with the huge booty that they were certain to obtain if they were successful. Ali Barid Shah was slightly overweight, with a pleasant face. He was smiling even though there was a hint of unease in it. Ali knew what the man was thinking, even with all of them combined, they would be hard pressed to defeat the armies of Samrajya and if they failed, the response would be swift. Ramaraya would make sure of that. Bidar with its small army and rather vulnerable position would have little chance of survival. Still the man was here, for which Ali was thankful. He glanced at the last seat, reserved for the Imad Shahi Sultan but the current occupant of the throne, Burhan Imad Shah was three, so his absence was not unexpected although the Imad Shahi force that had answered the call was rather underwhelming.

The prince's guardian Tufail Khan stood behind the empty throne. His hand placed over it with more than passing familiarity. Ali gave an inward sigh. I wonder how much longer the boy will be the Sultan, he mused. But it was a thought for another day, for today they only had a single reason of being there and that was discussing the battle plans, except it was late in the night and they were no closer to it than when they had begun.

"Do they think Ramaraya would spend so much time in idle posturing?" he thought annoyed. No, he knew the moment Ramaraya received their declaration of war, he would mobilise his armies for war immediately. And according to his estimates, the messenger would have arrived in Vijayanagara and delivered the message.

"Sultan Hussain Shah," Ali spoke, "What is your plan for the coming campaign?" he asked.

Hussain Nizam Shah regarded him and gave a broad smile, "We will march swiftly and cross Krishna River, forcing Ramaraya and his cowards to defend their lands. Once in their lands we can unleash our cavalry forces, that can attack towns and cities across the enemy lands. Ramaraya will despatch his forces to oppose us, but considering they will be dominated by infantry, we can run circles around them. If we siege Raichur, Mudgal and the remaining important towns simultaneously, Ramaraya would be forced to split his armies to aid the cities. When they do, we can destroy them one by one or simply march towards the enemy capital Vijayanagara. Let us see how Ramaraya will like it when his own capital is threatened."

"What happens if he decides to keep his army in the capital?"

"Well then he would have to explain to all his northern Nayakas on his failure to defend them."

"There won't be a lot of them left because we can capture most of their territories quickly if Ramaraya fails to send reinforcements." Tufail Khan added, looking pleased.

"It's a win for us either way, we will be able to capture significant enemy territory or if Ramaraya reacts as we hope he would; we can cut off the head of the snake by destroying Vijayanagara itself."

The bastard is thinking quite far into the future with this. Quite uncharacteristic for him, Ali mused, wondering whether Hussain Nizam Shah had come up with the plan. It did not matter, it was a decent plan and despite what Hussain Shah thought, the campaign would proceed quite different to the way Hussain Shah was hoping because Ali knew Ramaraya's mind better than anyone here and the old man would take the fight to his enemies.

******

# CHAPTER 2
# 1510

The chaos of the battle threatened to overwhelm him completely. It was not that Ramaraya was a virgin in the field of war, but he had never fought in a such a large-scale battle. More than one lakh soldiers were fighting that day, on the field of Diwani. Ramaraya felt like he too was one among the nameless mass of soldiers fighting to death in the name of their ruler and nation. He glanced back towards the main battle-line where a large force of war elephants had been stationed, surrounding a richly caparisoned beast. Atop it was the lord of Karnata Samrajya, the most powerful man south of Vindhyas, Emperor Krishnadevaraya. And he was fighting for his life today.

"Anna, they keep coming," Tirumala pointed grimly at a large force of enemy cavalry that smashed aside Samrajya infantry like dried leaves before a storm and were now bearing down upon the royal elephant, their intention rather clear.

Ramaraya looked around him, at the men waiting for his command. Most of them were his kinsmen and retainers of the Aravidu family and he was loathed to fling them at an enemy that appeared to be unstoppable. But as soldiers of the Samrajya, their duty was clear.

"Rama, we must do something before it's too late," his cousin Paparaya growled as the enemy cavalry kept creeping towards them.

"Tirumala you will ride behind me," Ramaraya commanded, turning his horse towards the enemy, not waiting for his brother's acknowledgement. He rode to the front ranks of his men as they formed two lines fifty feet apart.

*"With me, soldiers of Samrajya, for Aravidu Vamsha and for Krishnadevaraya!"* Ramaraya screamed, leading his forces in a furious counter charge. He gripped his lance tightly, his eyes focussed ahead on the enemy riders who continued their relentless advance. Ramaraya felt a momentary fear at what might be his last moments in the world.

"No, my story will not end here, not like this. I am destined to become a famous man in the history of Samrajya," Ramaraya promised himself.

He looked back at the approaching enemies and gave a predatory smile. "But it will be the last day for many of you. Because Ramaraya is going to make a name for himself today on your corpses."

The two lines were only hundred meters apart and the enemy fired their volley, the arrows missing Ramaraya, but he did hear a few of his men go down. Ramaraya's smile widened.

*"Govinda!"* Ramaraya cried.

*"Govinda!"* His men responded as they smashed into the enemy formation.

******

Ramaraya threw his last javelin at an enemy rider without success. He then drew his sword and fought a desperate struggle to keep the Shahi cavalry from the emperor's elephant.

*"Anna duck!"* came Tirumala's scream and Ramaraya threw his body down unthinkingly. A lucky decision as a sword passed over him just moments later where Ramaraya's head would have been if

not for Tirumala's warning. But his sudden movement had made his horse kneel in surprise, throwing Ramaraya to the ground. He was up quickly as he parried a swing by another enemy at his shoulder. Ramaraya punched the man in his jaw with his left hand. And before he could recover, he slashed at his neck leaving a gaping hole in his throat. He quickly located his horse and mounted back up, looking around for his men. He found Tirumala roaring at their few remaining men trying to reform them, but Ramaraya knew it was pointless. He looked at Paparaya, and his cousin gave Ramaraya a grim nod. Their attempts at halting the Shahis had failed and now the enemy had the freedom to attack the emperor and end this battle.

"What do we do?" Paparaya asked urgently. Ramaraya was about to respond when a war cry uttered by thousands of throats pierced through the noise of the battle.

*"Jai Virupaksha!"*

Ramaraya watched with amazement as thousands of royal cavalrymen charged towards him, their momentum enough to scatter the Shahi cavalry who were now widely dispersed.

Looks like the emperor is going to be safe, Ramaraya thought. He was about to order his men back to the defence of the emperor's elephant when his eyes fell upon the officer leading the Samrajya counter charge.

"I don't believe it!" he cried surprised as he looked once again at the royal elephant only to finally understand the emperor's plan. The man on the elephant was a fake and the emperor had let the enemy expend their strength in their attempts to kill the fake. He was even now leading his men on a decisive charge. As the emperor and his men passed him, Ramaraya gave a shake of his head in admiration of the man.

"We are following the emperor," he cried to Tirumala and Paparaya, not waiting to see if they followed him. Ramaraya had the opportunity to display his skills to the emperor in person and he did not intend to waste it.

"Today will be my day," he promised as he joined the royal cavalry men towards the enemy once again.

******

Where it had initially appeared that the enemy forces had been completely thrown off guard by Emperor Krishnadevaraya's tactics as the Samrajya cavalry ploughed deeper and deeper into the enemy formation, Ramaraya could see the enemy reforming, stiffening their lines to halt the Samrajya progress.

"Looks like it will be a longer day," Ramaraya thought tiredly as he willed his body to ride on despite being extremely tired. The emperor was only a few dozen feet ahead, fighting fiercely surrounded by his bodyguards. He appeared to be safe for now, but as the battle progressed, Ramaraya could see that there was danger that the emperor and his bodyguards could be overwhelmed.

As though confirming his fears, Ramaraya saw a large body of enemy riders throw themselves at the emperor's guard, two even managing to break through. The lead rider, a burly Abyssinian, closed in on the emperor, knocking down one of the emperor's bodyguards.

"*Tirumala come!*" Ramaraya cried, kicking his horse hard.

He watched the first Abyssinian being tackled by one of the emperor's bodyguards. But his companion closed in, killing the last bodyguard between him and the emperor. He then crashed his horse into the emperor's horse, throwing them both to the ground. The emperor was undaunted as he fought the enemy soldier on the ground, but another of the royal bodyguard, a young man, tackled the Abyssinian. They wrestled on the ground and Abyssinian gained the upper hand, squeezing the life out of the bodyguard. But the emperor quickly closed in on the pair and cut off the enemy soldier's head before he could kill the bodyguard. But in his haste to save his bodyguard, the emperor had failed to notice another rider bearing down upon him, his sword raised. Ramaraya cried in anger as he realised, he might not be able to reach the emperor in time.

"No, I will not miss this opportunity," he cried as he looked around the battlefield desperately. His eyes fell on a spear that was sticking from the ground. He rode hard and picked up the spear in a single motion. He barely had time to aim as the enemy rider was almost on top of the emperor, his sword raised high. Ramaraya threw the spear, praying to all the gods to let his aim be perfect. His prayers were answered, and the spear stuck the enemy rider, sending him sprawling to the ground. The emperor looked up and at Ramaraya,

"You are Aravidi Bukka's grandsons," he said nodding at the three.

Ramaraya bowed respectfully, but he kept an eye out for another attack. But as he scanned the battlefield, he realised that the enemy finally had enough and were now fleeing the battlefield in all directions.

"Prabhu, the battle is over; we are victorious!" one of the bodyguards cried. The men around screamed joyously.

The emperor raised his hand to halt the celebration.

"This is not over, not until we have chased back each of the sultans back to their own lands. I will go after Yusuf Adil Shah myself," the emperor cried, looking at each of his men.

His eyes rested upon Ramaraya.

"You saved my life. What do you desire, young man?" he asked.

Ramaraya felt a strange pleasure upon hearing those words. All his efforts until now had not been in vain.

"Mahaprabhu, please let us accompany you for the rest of the campaign," he said, making sure to keep his voice respectful.

His words must have pleased the emperor for he gave Ramaraya an approving nod, "Very well, you will ride by my side. We will go after Adil Shah immediately," he commanded.

Ramaraya bowed respectfully once again. He could see his cousin looking at him in confusion, no doubt wondering why Ramaraya had not asked for more.

Lands and wealth are dust compared to the gratitude of the emperor of Samrajya, he thought pleased at how the day had turned out.

******

Yusuf Adil Shah's flight for safety had ended disastrously. At the battle of Kovilkonda, the Sultan had been mortally injured, removing the greatest threat to Samrajya. With his victory at Diwani and then at Kovilkonda, the emperor had succeeded in ending the Shahi threat once and for all. A victory unmatched in the history of Samrajya, one worthy of being immortalised in the annals of Samrajya and Ramaraya had been given the honour of bearing the news of this triumph to the people of Vijayanagara. Ramaraya was nervous probably for the first time in his life. He glanced at his brother Tirumala who appeared to be as awed as Ramaraya. The city garrison had seen Ramaraya's approach, accompanied by the emperor's standard and the Samrajya royal emblem, both held high.

As he approached the city, the gates of the city were opened, and soldiers rushed to form a battle-line. A small group of riders approached Ramaraya, led by the city kotwal. The kotwal halted some distance away raising his right hand in a greeting.

"What news of our Mahaprabhu?" the kotwal asked looking tensed.

Ramaraya simply gave a broad smile, and he watched the kotwal's shoulders straighten quickly as he understood that Ramaraya carried good news.

"I carry news for the Rajaguru Vysatheertha from our emperor. Please take me to him."

The kotwal did not ask any more questions and he led Ramaraya and his men into the city. His passage did not go unnoticed as the people realised that Ramaraya carried news from the battlefield. As he neared the palace, a sea of people had come to watch him deliver the message. Vysatheertha stood at the entrance of the royal compound, his face serene. Ramaraya got down from his horse and bowed down to touch the Rajaguru's feet reverentially.

"Tell me my son, what news from our beloved emperor?"

Ramaraya felt as if he was the centre of all attention. Even though he stood surrounded by thousands of people, not a single sound could be heard, as if no one wanted to interrupt Ramaraya. Ramaraya took a deep breath, he had practised what he would say to the people multiple times along the journey.

"Five days ago, on the auspicious day of Chaturthi, the armies of Samrajya crushed the Turushka armies at Diwani and scattered them in all directions. Yusuf Adil Shah, the main instigator of the annual aggression against the Samrajya was mortally injured at Kovilkonda. The emperor has captured Raichur and Mudgal. The enemy sultans have all sent their envoys requesting for peace."

There was another few seconds of stunned silence as the enormity of the news finally sank into the minds of everyone. Then there came out a roar that appeared to shake the very heavens as the people of Vijayanagara went hysterical with joy.

******

Ramaraya felt as though he was living a dream as he and his men were paraded throughout the streets of Samrajya. It was as though, he, Ramaraya was the personification of the victory. Wherever he went, he was met with people who touched him almost reverentially, many even falling to his feet asking for his blessings. Ramaraya accompanied Vysatheertha to the Virupaksha temple, where the patron deity of the Samrajya was first established. As the priests began to perform a ceremony in honour of this great victory, Ramaraya was lost in his own thoughts. He had always felt he wished to leave his mark on Samrajya. He wanted people to remember him but never in his mind had he ever considered that he wanted to become more than a great general or a minister of the Samrajya. But today as he lapped up the adoration of the people, most of it he knew was directed towards the emperor, who realised that he was seeing the transformation of a man into a god. Krishnadevaraya had been transformed into a god in the minds of all the people of Samrajya after his great victory at Diwani. Not unlike how Immadi Devaraya was still worshipped by people of Samrajya as a great ruler and an enlightened soul, even a hundred years after his death. He had achieved lasting fame, immortality even. Ramaraya finally knew what he truly desired in his life.

******

# CHAPTER 3
# 1564

To be honest, Ramaraya was not truly surprised hearing that all the Shahi kingdoms had united to form an alliance against him and Samrajya. In fact, he had expected them to attempt that precise thing since it had become clear that the Samrajya forces were significantly more powerful than the army of any single Shahi kingdom. So, as he made for the war council, Ramaraya was not concerned. He had planned for this outcome, despite his brother Venkatadri's unease.

Today, the royal court was rather sparsely filled, only a dozen men were waiting for him. Ramaraya made his way to the raised platform upon which was a seat made of padded silk cushions. On it sat a purple kulavi. Ramaraya bowed dutifully at the seat. It was the seat of power of the Emperor of Samrajya, Sadashiva Raya, who would not attend the war council. Just beneath the raised platform was another slightly shorter platform, where another opulent seat made similarly of gilded silk cushions and precious jewels was kept. Ramaraya mounted the platform and sat down, he accepted the thambula from his betel bearer, popping it into his mouth and chewing it slowly, enjoying the taste. He smiled at the betel bearer,

"You have done well; the leaves are especially tender today."

"I am not worthy of such high praise, Prabhu," he said bowing.

"A hundred gold coins for Thimma Nayudu," Ramaraya announced, waiting for a few minutes for the scribe to note down his command. That done, Ramaraya turned his attention back to the assembled men.

"Tirumala?" he smiled at his brother.

"Prabhu, we are ready to march to the borders tomorrow morning."

"We will be leading thirty thousand infantry, five thousand cavalry and a hundred elephants, Peddananna," Raghunatha added.

"Good, that should give you a strong core force," Ramaraya said. "I am also granting you, Tirumala, the authority to command the forces of all of the Nayakas around the Krishna river in my stead," he said, once again waiting for the scribe to write down the order. Soon it would be copied and despatched via messengers to all of the Nayakas, informing them of Ramaraya's order.

"Prabhu, we have also sent forth messengers to all of the Nayakas ordering them to lead their forces to the capital within two months," Raghunatha added.

Ramaraya glanced at his brother Venkatadri and the two brothers shared an unspoken conversation. Both knew that two months would not be enough to assemble the vast host of Samrajya. Especially the forces of the most powerful Nayakas, who ruled over the Tamil lands and Canara coast. They would take much longer to arrive due to the vast distances from the capital. But still, Ramaraya was satisfied by the order as it would ensure at least the other Nayakas would arrive on time.

"Have we sent envoys to the other Shahis, asking them not be involved in the struggle?"

"We have sent them, Prabhu, but we do not expect them to succeed," Venkatadri said.

"No, but hopefully they will make our enemies think we are scared and delay their preparations. The longer we delay this battle, the more certain our victory," Ramaraya declared. Everyone in the hall nodded at that accurate. If the Samrajya could mobilise its full force, comprising of all its Nayakas, then the Shahis did not stand a chance.

"Then I will not delay further, Anna," Tirumala said, not trying to hide his enthusiasm.

"Go Tirumala, may Lord Virupaksha be with you," Ramaraya commanded. As his brother turned to leave, "Remember Tirumala, your job is to prevent the enemy from crossing the river. I will come with reinforcements within a month. Do not let them provoke you to any rash actions," he said sternly looking at Raghunatha.

"We understand our orders, Peddananna. We will maintain our positions and prevent the enemy from crossing the river," Raghunatha promised with a bow.

Once they left, Ramaraya turned to his brother Venkatadri, "You will be responsible for putting together the reinforcements, brother."

"As you command, Prabhu," Venkatadri bowed.

"The meeting is dismissed," Ramaraya declared standing up.

"Prepare the steam room," he told Thimma Naidu.

******

They should have been at the banks of Krishna by now, instead they were still camped outside Bijapur, supposedly waiting for more troops. But Ali's fears were growing as the days went on. It was a view many of his senior commanders shared as well.

"Huzoor, our spies have reported back," Kishwar Khan told Ali in his tent.

"Let me guess, Ramaraya has despatched a large force under his brother Venkatadri to garrison the forts along the river Krishna,"

Ali sighed.

"You are correct, Huzoor. A large force but under his other brother Tirumala," Kishawar Khan replied.

"What does that mean, Huzoor? Why send the lesser experienced brother?" Abu Shirazi asked worried. Ali almost laughed seeing his friend's discomfort as the worried expression seemed strangely out of place on Abu's cherubic face.

"It means Ramaraya is preparing a second, larger army to send later under Venkatadri's command," Ali said thoughtfully.

"What kind of force does Tirumala command?" Abu asked.

"Some thirty thousand infantry and five thousand cavalry and a hundred elephants."

"That's a sizable force."

"It will be larger since I am sure Tirumala will start to levy soldiers from all the Nayakas around Krishna," Ali said calmly.

"That will swell their numbers dangerously," Kishawar Khan warned.

"They are levies, the only thing they will add is numbers," Ali said contemptuously. "No, it's the second army under Venkatadri that should concern us."

"Huzoor, the Nayakas from the south would still need many months to reach the capital. If we attack now, we should be able to stop the enemy from concentrating its full army," Abu said.

"If I can convince that pompous fool, oops," Ali grinned without any humour. "I meant my esteemed father-in-law, the great Hussain Shah to hurry up, then we have a good chance."

"Perhaps he is right in waiting for more men, Huzoor; it might help to even the odds," Abu suggested.

"That is a game we will never win, Abu. We will never be able to match the Samrajya numbers. The longer we wait, defeat will be more likely. No, our only chance of success lies in forcing the engagement swiftly."

"But how will we convince the other sultans?" Kishawar Khan asked.

"I will convince them, but I am worried that it might be too late," Ali sighed.

******

Ramaraya walked back to his chamber from the steam room, his chest feeling lighter. He took a deep breath, enjoying the feeling of air filling his lungs completely. He had started to notice that lately his breathing had become more laborious. The physicians had tried everything without success and only an hour in the steam room could give Ramaraya some relief.

"How much longer do I have?" he wondered, not really wishing for an answer, but he could guess that it probably wasn't very long. The thought did not upset him. He had led a long and successful life and achieved everything that he had set out for himself.

"Everything?" he asked himself as the familiar ache in his chest reminded him of his greatest unfulfilled desire.

He mused about the new and soon to be ill-fated attempt by the Shahis to change the balance of power. Everyone in the court considered the coming war as a serious danger to Samrajya, but Ramaraya knew better. It was an opportunity provided by the gods to fulfil his dream at last.

The guards at the door straightened at his approach.

"Prabhu, Mahadevi Mohanagi is in your chambers waiting for you," one of them declared.

Ramaraya brightened on hearing the words. He had missed her company the last few months.

She was sitting with her back to him, her hands moving over the veena with practised proficiency. Ramaraya stood for several minutes listening to the exquisite music. He was a good player of the veena himself, but could never become as good as his wife. A thought that made Ramaraya envious of his wife often. She stopped suddenly as if noticing Ramaraya's presence. She stood up quickly, greeting Ramaraya with a shy smile. Like always, Ramaraya felt his breath taken away when his eyes fell upon his wife. The long years had done nothing to mar her beauty, and for Ramaraya she was just as beautiful today as the first time he laid eyes on her.

"Swami," she said touching his feet reverentially.

Ramaraya hugged her gently.

"How was your trip?" he asked.

"It was pleasant."

"I thought you were planning to stay longer at Chandragiri."

"That's one way of saying you are not too keen to see me, Swami," she said playfully.

Ramaraya laughed, "On the contrary, I was eagerly waiting for you."

Immediately Mohanagi's manner became serious which told Ramaraya that his wife knew about the threat that Samrajya faced.

"Why is Ali doing this? He always called me mother," she asked upset.

"And he probably truly considers you as such," Ramaraya said gently.

"Then why is he joining the alliance against us?" Mohanagi asked in a disturbed voice.

Ramaraya gave her a sad smile, "Ali truly values his relationship with us dear, but he also understands that this is the only opportunity for Bijapur to assert itself and take the place of Bahmani Sultanate as the strongest state in the Deccan."

"Replacing Samrajya?"

"That is Ali's ambition and I do not hold it against him. I would have done the same in his place."

"Swami, surely we can avoid this war."

"No," Ramaraya shook his head. "I did not desire for this war, but I will not back away from it."

"Why, Swami?"

"Because don't you see? This is my chance at last, one final opportunity to surpass your father."

She understood it, better than anyone else. She understood his anger and frustration.

"He made a mistake, Swami," she said and Ramaraya knew that she meant it. She had been his greatest strength during those dark days.

"It does not matter, but everyone in Samrajya knows that the great Krishnadevaraya never considered me worthy enough to be his successor. Everything I have done until now pales in comparison to his achievement. But if I can end the threat of the Shahis once and for all, then maybe, maybe I will finally find my place among the great rulers of Samrajya."

Ramaraya saw Mohanagi wanted to argue further, but she did not instead she gave a tired smile.

"I will pray for your victory, Swami," she declared and Ramaraya fell in love with his wife all over again.

"Sit, I would like to hear you play the veena today," he said.

Mohanagi sat down and placed the veena on her lap. Ramaraya was engrossed in the melodious music, his worries and ambitions momentarily forgotten.

******

# CHAPTER 4
# 1515

"Odeya, should we pull him out?"

Ramaraya watched the figures struggling in the distance, trying to save themselves from drowning in the strong waters of river Cauvery. Two small coracle boats were making their way towards the drowning men but the eyes of the men inside the boat were not upon the men in the water; instead they were looking at Ramaraya who stood at the ramparts of the fort observing them.

Gangaraja, the lord of Shivanasamudra, had attempted to secede from Samrajya and in response the Samrajya had sent Aravidu Bukka, Ramaraya's grandfather to crush the man. A year long siege had culminated in storming of Gangaraja's Island fortress with its master now attempting to flee using the river. Except his little boat had capsized and he was now at the mercy of Ramaraya's men who had followed him.

"Odeya?" the voice asked once more, assuming Ramaraya had not heard the first time.

"If we pull Gangaraja out of the river, he will be grateful for all of six months before going back to his old ways of a rebel."

"Odeya, your grandfather commanded us to capture Gangaraja alive if possible."

Ramaraya glared at the man who visibly flinched at the gaze. “Odeya I...” he tried.

“I know what my grandfather said, Virappa,” he growled. “But I am still trying to decide whether Gangaraja has any use in the future.”

“To whom, Odeya?” Virappa asked, his eyes not daring to meet Ramaraya’s gaze.

Ramaraya placed a hand on the man’s shoulder, “Samrajya’s” he lied.

“He is a senior Nayaka of the Samrajya.”

“Who has rebelled one too many times,” Ramaraya smiled harshly. “I think I have made my decision; I don’t wish to ever come back to Shivanasamudra again. My future is in Vijayanagara. Gangaraja has served his purpose to me and Samrajya. Signal Bisalappa and the men.”

“As you command, Odeya. I will ask them to withdraw. Gangaraja will drown in some time,” Virappa said.

Ramaraya’s grip on his shoulders tightened, “Withdraw?” he demanded. “You misunderstand, Virappa. I do not wish to leave Gangaraja’s fate in the hands of the gods. Signal Bisalappa to drown the bastards himself. And you will stay and make sure that each one of them is properly drowned.”

“Odeya,” Virappa said bowing, his face white.

Ramaraya gave him a cheerful smile, “Good, I will return to the camp to give grandfather the tragic news myself. We are returning to Vijayanagara.”

******

He was richly rewarded for the victory over Gangaraja with the lordship of Chandragiri fortress, one of the richest fiefs in Samrajya. Yet it only made Ramaraya hungrier. Ramaraya watched his warriors practise their daily cavalry manoeuvres with undisguised pride. He had modelled them after the royal cavalry of Samrajya and Ramaraya had not spared any expense to equip them with the best weapons and armour. Their numbers were still woefully low, but he could not increase their numbers drastically without it being perceived as a threat by the emperor. No, Ramaraya was content to wait for the chance to increase the numbers of his *Rachebidas*. Today, however, he seemed to have an audience, an unwanted one according to Ramaraya. His cousin Paparaya had appeared at the training grounds without warning. Ramaraya wondered the reason for Paparaya's sudden appearance after he had spent the last several months avoiding Ramaraya.

Paparaya had not spoken much, instead his eyes were fixed upon the Rachebidas with undisguised avariciousness.

"Are we going to watch until the end before you tell me the reason for your visit, cousin?" Ramaraya asked accepting a beeda from a servant.

"Sorry about that, cousin, but I have not seen another force comparable to your Rachebidas in skill."

Is this your attempts at winning my support? Ramaraya thought amused.

Paparaya thought he was a genius at manipulation, but his methods were too obvious to all, but the most stupid.

"Thank you, cousin, it took me only three years to train them," he replied carefully.

"You have always been committed, Rama. That is your best quality," Paparaya smiled.

He really must want something very badly, decided Ramaraya, amused.

"The emperor has appointed a minister as the viceroy of the province of Shivanasamudra," Paparaya said suddenly.

"I know. I was there," Ramaraya nodded.

"By rights, it should have been given to our Aravidu family. We were responsible for defeating the rebel," Paparaya declared.

*You* were enjoying at Vijayanagara while grandfather and I did all the work, the words almost came to Ramaraya, but he agreed with his cousin's assessment. While it was the right of the emperor to allot the fief to any Nayaka he saw fit, it was generally accepted that the Nayaka who led the forces in the actual campaign had the first right upon it. Quite a few of the Aravidu family vassals who took part in the campaign had voiced their displeasure to Ramaraya.

"The emperor must have his reason," Ramaraya said carefully.

"And we are the most powerful Nayaka family in Samrajya."

"What are you implying, cousin?" Ramaraya demanded as he made eye contact with his bodyguard Bisalappa, who quickly walked away from Ramaraya and his cousin. The other guards did the same, making sure that no one was within hearing range of them.

"Are you in agreement with the emperor's decision, cousin?"

Ramaraya's eyes narrowed. Does the fool understand what he is saying? He is suggesting treason, Ramaraya thought shocked.

"He is the emperor, Papa," he said simply.

"When the emperor's brother Vira Narasimha was insulted by the last Saluva emperor, Immadi Narasimha, he was disposed by nobles led by Vira Narasimha. The Tuluva family became the new emperors of Samrajya."

"Careful cousin, your words are straying dangerous territory," Ramaraya warned.

"I am simply stating a fact, Rama. The Tuluva family owe their rise to the Nayaka families of Samrajya, but the emperor seems to have forgotten."

"Papa..."

"I know you aspire to be more than a simple Nayaka, Rama. I can see the hunger in your eyes."

"I don't..." Ramaraya began angrily.

"Come to my house tomorrow evening. I want you to meet a few people. They need to discuss a few things with you,"

"And what exactly are we discussing?" Ramaraya asked carefully.

"Tomorrow evening, do not be late," Paparaya said standing up. He took out a bag of gold from his waist and threw it at the Rachebidas troopers who had finished their training and were now walking their horses back to the stable.

They are *my* soldiers, not common whores! Ramaraya almost roared at Paparaya, but he managed to keep his temper. Virappa bent down and picked up the bag and walked towards them.

"Prabhu, you must have dropped your bag of gold," he said handing the bag back to Paparaya.

Ramaraya watched Paparaya's confusion at the soldier rejecting his 'gift'. His eyes narrowed and before he could lose his temper, Ramaraya stood up and took the bag from the soldier's hands.

"My cousin has generously decided to reward every Rachebida with gold for their skills and bravery."

"Odeya, your trust is all that we desire. We thank Paparaya Prabhu for his benevolence," Virappa declared bowing.

Paparaya raised his head haughtily, "Well done," he said before walking away.

Ramaraya waited for Paparaya to leave, then he threw the bag of gold to a servant.

"Take that and ask my *karyakarta* to buy manure for my lands with it," he growled, his eyes fixed upon Paparaya.

******

Emperor Krishnadevaraya, after his decisive victory over the Turushkas had joined the annals of history as one of the greatest emperors of Samrajya. A demigod worshipped by the common people and more importantly, according to Ramaraya, commanding an undefeated and fanatically loyal military of Samrajya.

"And Paparaya thinks that all it would take is two dozen disgruntled noblemen to overthrow the emperor," Ramaraya sighed. He had little confidence in his cousin's ability, but still he was hopeful that Paparaya and his 'conspirators' would come up with at least a feasible plan. Instead, he found the gathering high on energy and not much on anything else. Which was rather sad since Ramaraya knew that Paparaya's assessment of discontent among the Nayakas was accurate. But Paparaya proved too incompetent to take advantage of it. Worse, he and his 'conspirators' had also been discovered. The emperor and Mahamantri Timmarasu had taken a note of their activities. Ramaraya had learned the fact in the most direct way that very morning when Emperor Krishnadevaraya had called Ramaraya to the palace and had asked him to 'spy' on his cousin. Ramaraya did not doubt that his cousin's rebellion would fail, but he was worried about the repercussion on the Aravidu family. But he had agreed to spy on his cousin, which was why he was attending their 'revolutionary' meeting that day.

"We can all start rebellions simultaneously in our *Amarams* forcing the royal army to split up. That should weaken the forces in the capital for a direct strike on the emperor."

Ramaraya saw many of them nodding their heads as though the plan was a good one instead of what it was – plain suicide.

"Time to nip this in the bud. If I succeed in showing them the truth, maybe our family can survive Paparaya's actions," Ramaraya decided.

"It won't work," he said loudly. "The royal army is head and shoulders more capable than any of the Nayaka forces. They would make quick work of your men."

That was not well received as many of them glared at Ramaraya.

"You have a rather high opinion of the royal army, Ramaraya," someone commented.

"Yes, I do, because I was present at the battle of Diwani. If there is anyone here who thinks that his household forces are a match for the Turushka cavalry, I would like to know. The royal army has defeated them, not once but multiple times. The Turushkas are no longer raiding our lands because they fear to engage our armies in battle."

"If we wanted to hear emperor's praise, we would have attended the royal court," a young man, barely in his teens retorted.

"You could have, before the guards at the door would have turned you away," Ramaraya laughed.

"Cousin, are you here to provoke us?" Paparaya asked carefully.

"I am here to hear your plan, Papa, and I haven't heard one until now," he responded.

Paparaya did not reply but Ramaraya could see him considering his words. "As this is my cousin's first meeting, it's natural that he is wary," he laughed. "We will meet again in two days."

The place quickly emptied leaving only Ramaraya and his cousin.

"You are right, Rama," Paparaya said suddenly. "That was a rather poor plan."

"Papa, what are you doing?" Ramaraya demanded. "When you spoke to me yesterday, I assumed you had gained the support of many of the senior Nayakas."

"We are working on it, Rama," Papa tried to assure him, his smile widening.

"You cannot wait for long, Papa, How long before the emperor learns of your plan?"

"Maybe he already has," Papa replied, his eyes narrowing at Ramaraya. "I heard you went to the palace today."

Ramaraya was taken aback for a moment, "I had to. I was summoned," he said calmly.

"I know," Papa continued to smile but there was no warmth in it. "What did the emperor wish to speak to you about?"

"He wanted me to make a sacrifice," Ramaraya replied as a plan started forming in his head.

"What kind of sacrifice?"

"He wants me to step down as the Amaranayaka of Chandragiri. He wishes to place it under the care of a Durgadandanayaka."

"And you agreed?" Paparaya demanded angrily.

"You think I have a choice?"

"Do you see? Did I not tell you cousin, that he has forgotten who his allies are?"

Ramaraya shrugged, trying to appear helpless.

"Never mind, Ajja will be angrier now."

"Ajja knows about you?" Ramaraya asked shocked.

"Of course, do you think I wouldn't tell him?"

"He has agreed to your insurrection?"

"I even have his seal to command our household troops when we finally make our move."

This cannot be happening, Ramaraya thought staggered as the full scope of his family's involvement became apparent.

"Paparaya, are we the only ones?" he asked moistening his mouth.

"For now, but we have already despatched messengers to one person who would definitely join us."

"Who?"

"Gajapati Prataparudra. You are correct, Rama, we cannot overcome the royal army by splitting them into smaller units, but what if Samrajya is attacked by an external enemy?"

"The emperor will lead the forces in person," Ramaraya said.

"Correct, and you will accompany him along with your men. He trusts you Rama, and in heat of battle, a lot can happen," Paparaya grinned meaningfully.

"What about you?" Ramaraya asked.

"I will lead our forces to capture Vijayanagara and crown our grandfather as the new emperor. The Aravidu family will ascend the throne as the rightful heirs of Samrajya," Paparaya said grinning like a little boy.

Ramaraya was too shocked to respond, and he only managed to respond with a weak smile of his own.

******

Ramaraya did not return home. Instead, he headed to a place where he should have gone in the first place. He was not stopped as he entered the large compound. He looked at the head of the guards who recognised him immediately.

"Prabhu, he is in the gardens," the man indicated.

Ramaraya turned left and walked through an arch and towards a large garden. He found the man he had come to meet on his knees, digging the ground with a small shovel. He looked up at Ramaraya and gave a broad smile standing up to his full height. He was several inches taller than Ramaraya and despite being in his sixties, Aravidu Bukka's posture was erect.

"Rama," he waved him nearer.

Ramaraya touched his grandfather's feet reverentially.

"*Taathaiya,*" he said.

"You have almost stopped coming, Rama. Have I done something that caused you to avoid your grandfather?" he asked.

"No, Taathaiya, I have been busy," he replied. Aravidi Bukka peered at Ramaraya,

"What is the matter, boy?" he asked slowly.

Ramaraya glanced around, noticing several of the guards within earshot.

"Come, I have to show you something. I have managed to grow a flowering plant that is supposed to flower only in China," he said, placing his left hand on Ramaraya's shoulder and leading him forward.

"What is the matter?" he asked again in a low voice.

"Paparaya," Ramaraya said looking sideways at his grandfather.

"What about him?"

"He is making a mistake," Ramaraya said simply.

"The emperor is the one making a mistake," Aravidu Bukka said sounding annoyed.

They stood in front of a small shrub that was beginning to bear strikingly red flowers.

"It's beautiful," Ramaraya said examining the petals softly.

"Isn't it?" Aravidu Bukka beamed.

"Paparaya has sent a messenger asking for aid," Ramaraya said still looking at the flower.

"Who to?"

"Gajapati Prataparudra," Ramaraya said taking a step back and facing his grandfather.

"He what?" Aravidu Bukka's eyes nearly fell from his face, which confirmed Ramaraya's suspicion that Paparaya had not informed their grandfather of his updated plan.

"That stupid reckless child," Aravidu Bukka cursed.

"The emperor and Mantri Timmarasu know," Ramaraya continued.

His grandfather's face was white now.

"I..."

"What were you thinking, Taathaiya?" Ramaraya asked angrily.

"Rama, we are the Aravidu family. We were responsible for the rise of Saluva Narasimha. Without us, Vira Narasimha could not have gained power, nor Krishnadevaraya could have ascended the throne without incident," his grandfather's voice rose higher.

"And will we take revenge by selling out Samrajya to the Gajapatis? Will the common people accept us? Will the other Nayaka families bow down to traitors?"

His grandfather staggered as if Ramaraya had slapped him.

"I..." there were tears in his eyes.

"Taathaiya, our family will rise to the highest position in Samrajya but not like this," Ramaraya said, gently wiping his grandfather's tears.

"I will ask Paparaya to go into exile," his grandfather said sadly.

"It's too late for that. Paparaya's messenger will not go far, and he still has your letter authorising our soldiers to follow his command."

"What do you want me to do, Rama?"

Ramaraya hugged his grandfather tightly,

"Do you trust me?" he asked softly.

"With my life and our family's."

"Then trust me, grandfather."

Aravidu Bukka nodded weakly.

"I need the command of our household guards," Ramaraya said. His grandfather only could give a weak nod.

Ramaraya walked back outside the compound where his Rachebidas were waiting, dressed for battle.

"Odeya," Bisalappa said.

Ramaraya glanced back at a regiment of Aravidu soldiers coming up from inside the compound.

"Have you gotten the names of all of them?" Ramaraya asked.

"Odeya," Virappa nodded taking out a small scroll.

"Good, carry out your duties. For Samrajya and Aravidu family," Ramaraya declared. The men bowed and split into multiple groups, except the two dozen men with Bisalappa.

"We have work to do, Bisalappa," Ramaraya said simply, leading his men into the dark.

******

Paparaya woke up with a start, the sound of battle shattering the calm of the night. He sat up on the bed.

*"Servant!"* he roared, but there was no response.

"Kesavan, where are you, you useless—" he stopped mid-sentence as his eyes fell on the figure standing in the corner hidden by the night.

"Who?"

Ramaraya took a step forward, letting the moonlight light his face.

"Rama?" Paparaya appeared to be at a loss for words. But he soon recovered himself, his left hand slipping behind his pillow.

"Don't, you have no hope of bettering me in a duel?" Ramaraya said calmly.

"Why betray your own family?" Paparaya asked.

Ramaraya opened his mouth to respond when Bisalappa burst in led by a few soldiers.

"Done?" Ramaraya asked keeping his eyes fixed on Paparaya.

"Odeya, they are all dead."

Ramaraya nodded as he took another step towards Paparaya.

"Papa, I promise you that your dream that Aravidu family becomes the first family of Samrajya will be fulfilled. I will make it happen," he declared.

Paparaya's eyes moved from Ramaraya to the guards, some of them wearing the uniform of Aravidu family.

"The letter is in my desk, under a false bottom," he said. "Tell Taathaiya I am sorry for everything."

Ramaraya gave a sad smile.

"Did I have a chance?" Paparaya asked.

Ramaraya shook his head.

"I should have brought you in the beginning," he sighed, tears forming in his eye now.

"Goodbye, cousin," Ramaraya said walking towards the door. He did not trust himself that he would not succumb to weakness seeing his cousin's tears and fail in his duty. He stopped beside Bisalappa.

"If my cousin's courage fails, I need you to help him," Ramaraya said looking him squarely in the eye.

"Odeya," Bisalappa nodded.

In the main hall, his men were placing a dozen bodies at different places. All of them dressed in blackened armour.

Virappa stood nursing an injury on his arm. Seeing Ramaraya he stood erect.

"Odeya, it's done," he said.

A piercing scream came from the bedroom, making everyone turn towards it.

Ramaraya felt a single tear streak down his cheek.

"Yes, you are right, let us head back," he said softly.

******

Ramaraya noticed that his grandfather was in a rather joyous mood that day as he arrived at Ramaraya's home unannounced. Ramaraya touched his grandfather's feet respectfully.

"Taathaiya, you look happy, where are you coming from?"

"From the palace. The emperor invited me to have lunch with him."

Ramaraya held his breath. More than a week had passed since his night-time purge of all the conspirators. Under Ramaraya's direction, his grandfather had informed the palace that the Aravidu soldiers were forced to act against the conspirators after Paparaya had been killed. He had been trusted by the Aravidu family to get to the bottom of the conspiracy. It was a lie and Ramaraya was worried that the emperor or Mahamantri Timmarasu may not be convinced.

"What did the emperor say?"

"He agreed for our request to allow Paparaya's son to inherit his father's Amaram."

That surprised Ramaraya as granting Paparaya's Amaram to his son meant the emperor had accepted their explanation.

"We did it then," Ramaraya said relieved.

"Yes, we managed to escape unscathed, except for poor Paparaya," Aravidu Bukka said bitterly. His grandfather had still not forgiven Ramaraya for sacrificing his cousin.

"I had no choice, Taathaiya. He chose his fate," Ramaraya said testily.

"There was always a choice. He was family, Rama," Aravidu Bukka snapped.

Ramaraya did not reply.

"But that is not why I am here today," Aravidu Bukka said regaining his smile. "The emperor has decided to reward the family for our services."

"Reward us?" Ramaraya repeated.

"Yes, he wishes to establish a matrimonial alliance with our family."

"That is actually very good news," Ramaraya said happily. "Who has the emperor selected to be his bride?"

"The emperor does not wish to marry a girl from our family, Rama. He is offering the hand of his eldest daughter, Mohanagi."

Ramaraya's eyebrows rose as he realised what a great opportunity it would be for the Aravidu family.

"Who has been given the honour?"

"Who else?" his grandfather's smile widened. "The emperor Krishnadevaraya has offered the hand of his daughter to you."

"Me?" Ramaraya said shocked. He staggered and placed his hand on the wall nearby to steady himself.

"Rama, are you listening? Say something," Aravidu Bukka said, grasping Ramaraya's arm, concerned.

But for once in his life, Ramaraya felt speechless as his mind reeled at the announcement.

******

# CHAPTER 5
# 1564

"We should be marching," Ali declared shaking his head to the servant who offered him grapes. The servant moved to Hussain Shah, who picked up a bunch and put one into his mouth.

"Why?" he asked sucking on the grape, a surprised expression on his face. "Is this because Ramaraya has sent a force under his brother to garrison the forts?"

"Isn't that obvious?" Ali wanted to respond but instead he kept the smile plastered on his lips, which he was finding harder to maintain. "Yes," he said simply.

"You worry unnecessarily, Sultan Adil Shah. Our heavy cavalry will scatter the enemy in a single charge," he laughed plucking another grape with his teeth. Ali looked at Ibrahim Qutb Shah for support. Ibrahim had been silent most of the time like before, listening to their arguments, without weighing in. He hoped today would be different. Ali wanted to march but Hussain Shah did not, while the other sultans had pretty much not voted one way or the other. They were at an impasse.

"I think Sultan Adil Shah is right. No doubt our heavy cavalry will scatter the enemies, but they are also our most precious resource. We should not be so casual in using them. It is better we catch the enemy during his act of fortification." Ibrahim Qutb Shah said suddenly.

"I am still waiting for the second batch of mercenaries from Kandahar. They should arrive in a few weeks. Then we can march with full force." Hussain Nizam Shah responded, continuing to eat nonchalantly.

"We cannot wait that long as my spies have reported that Samrajya forces are not just occupying the forts along the river, they are also building new ones." Ali tried.

"Well, the fear of death does make one laborious. They know what awaits them, so they are trying to hide behind walls. It will do them no good," Hussain Shah laughed.

"It might cost us thousands of men," Ali warned.

"Once again, I agree with Sultan Adil Shah," Ibrahim added.

"But the mercenaries I am waiting for are all veterans of multiple battles. Their skill and experience will be invaluable," Hussain Shah responded.

"Huzoor, maybe we can do both," Kizzar Khan suggested.

"How?" Ali asked turning his head backward.

"We can send a portion of our cavalry south. They will attack the forts, kill enemy patrols and goad the enemy to chase them across the river. It will give them less opportunity to fortify themselves."

"Will *that* not be a waste of lives?" Hussain Shah demanded.

Ali opened his mouth to reply, but Ibrahim spoke first, "An acceptable loss, Sultan. We have a greater numbers and quality of cavalry. We can afford to lose two horsemen for a single enemy horseman. But without their cavalry, the enemy will be easy to defeat."

"Their cavalry are no longer elite units, not compared to what it was during the reign of Krishnadevaraya. Those men would have been very tough opponents," Hussain Shah replied, putting all the remaining grapes into his mouth.

"Yes, lucky for us," Ali declared, which brought laughter from quite a few in the tent. That was one of the only mistakes that Ali felt Ramaraya had made during his reign.

******

"If you need to ask me anything further, do not hesitate," Hussain Nizam Shah said in his customarily cheery self.

"You are very kind, Huzoor," Rumi Khan replied.

"Do you need help to carry them?" Hussain Shah asked indicating the two large bags in the corner.

"Asif and I will manage, Huzoor," Rumi Khan told him. He picked up one of the bags and hoisted it on his shoulders. It was extremely heavy, nearly fifty kilograms. But Rumi Khan's profession was a gunner and he had taken to the profession very young. He had built up the muscles required to wrestle the large guns into a proper firing position. Thus, carrying the heavy bag was not hard for him.

"Huzoor..." Asif hissed.

"Not here," Rumi Khan snapped as the two carried the bags to Rumi Khan's tent. Once inside, he dumped the bag unceremoniously into the corner along with more bags of the same sort.

"I have worked for many cheap rulers, but Hussain Nizam Shah is in a whole different league," Rumi Khan growled angrily, pouring himself a glass of wine. He watched Asif fish through the contents of the bag before throwing his hands up in disgust.

"There are only copper coins here," he said.

"Just like all the bags of 'payment' that we have received since the last six months," Rumi Khan spit the wine to the ground. "Even the wine is of cheap quality," he sighed.

"We should not have come here. We could have stayed in Rum and made a much larger sum," Asif said, voicing the opinion of many of Rumi Khan's men.

"You were there when his representatives visited us, and you heard the money that he promised, which was five times more than what we would earn with our old employer."

"Well, that is true," Asif laughed. "And he is truly a man of his word. We are being paid the quoted amount. Even though it's only in copper."

"Five times of zero is still zero," Rumi Khan responded angrily. Hussain Nizam Shah had hired rather massive number of troops from all over the world in a short time. As such, his only means of paying them was by minting more coins. With gold and silver long gone, Hussain Nizam Shah had taken to minting copper coins. As a result, the coins had pretty much become worthless.

"What should we do, Huzoor?"

"What else? See this expedition till the end and hope that after we win the battle, there will be enough plunder like what we have been promised," he replied.

*****

"Huzoor, I don't think Sarvadhikari Ramaraya should hire the two traitors," Ahmed commented softly in his ear. Venkatadri did not turn his head, his eyes fixed on the two men who were even now accepting beeda from his brother's hand.

"We hereby solemnly swear our loyalty and that of our men to Ramaraya and Samrajya," they declared.

Venkatadri saw a few frowning faces in the audience at the absence of the emperor's name, but they were few and far between.

"Excellent," Ramaraya beamed. "If you and your men perform admirably in the coming battle, then I will guarantee that you will receive the first pick of the spoils from the enemy."

That made quite a few people upset.

What are you doing Anna? Venkatadri thought, frustrated. The two men bowed once more and moved to the side to stand with the other commanders.

"Venkatadri, what news have we heard from Tirumala?" Ramaraya asked in a loud voice.

Venkatadri took a few steps to stand in front of his brother. He bowed quickly.

"Our men have started to fortify all the forts; the enemy's plans to invade will be foiled," he said loudly. His words set multiple inaudible conversations in the hall. Many wondering if there would even be a war now that Samrajya had successfully beaten the enemy to the river. Some even hoped that the enemy might see reason and would retreat to their lands.

"Silence!" Ramaraya commanded looking all around the hall.

"The meeting is concluded for today," Ramaraya declared. Venkatadri stood in his spot, he signalled Ahmed with a gaze to remain in the hall. Ramaraya too remained seated as if expecting Venkatadri to speak with him.

"Well brother," Ramaraya asked coolly.

Venkatadri nodded at Ahmed who bowed respectfully at Ramaraya.

"You wish to say something, Senanayaka?" Ramaraya asked.

"Huzoor, those two men cannot be trusted. They have changed their allegiance three times in less than half a decade," he warned.

"A fact they have not tried to hide," Ramaraya pointed out.

"Anna, what is stopping them from changing sides once more?"

"They have already made it clear that their loyalty is to the highest bidder and at this moment, no one can outbid Samrajya. You worry too much, Venkatadri. The Gilani brothers and their men will be a valuable addition to our forces. Especially in the coming war."

"It would be better if we rely on our own forces instead on mercenarics," Venkatadri said.

"We would have if we had the forces, as you very well know, Venkatadri".

"And who is responsible for that, Anna?" Venkatadri retorted.

His brother's face went cold at that, "Enough Venkatadri," Ramaraya replied angrily. "We have always used mercenaries during wars, and they have always been worth their weight in gold."

"Except when they aren't," Venkatadri replied in a tired voice. He was finding it harder to argue with his brother these days.

"You are tired brother, get some rest," Ramaraya commanded. Venkatadri bowed and left the hall along with Ahmed.

******

"Prabhu, shall I send word to get the steam bath ready?" Bisalappa asked.

Ramaraya did not reply. Sitting on his seat, his chin resting his left palm, he considered Venkatadri's words.

"He is right and wrong, you know," he said slowly.

"Odeya?"

"He is right, a powerful royal army would have come handy today. Except it was a huge drain on our resources. Our royal army grew from its modest numbers under Emperor Harihara Raya to its peak under Krishnadevaraya with a force of twenty thousand cavalry, one thousand elephants and one lakh infantry. We used to spend more than a quarter of the entire revenue of Samrajya on their maintenance. Under Achyutaraya, the army grew even larger, but lost its potency. Should I have continued to spend lavish amounts on them for little returns?"

Bisalappa was silent, as if waiting for Ramaraya to finish his musings.

"The Samrajya under me has expanded to cover more territory than even under the great Krishnadevaraya. And I have done it by spending Samrajya wealth judiciously. Do you think the successes I have achieved using diplomacy have been any less?" he looked at Bisalappa.

"Odeya, your achievements are not in any way lesser than Emperor Krishnadevaraya," Bisalappa responded instantly. It was a predictable response probably, but with Bisalappa, Ramaraya knew he meant it.

"If only everyone in Samrajya truly understood my efforts," he thought bitterly. Once again, he mastered his emotions by reminding himself that he had finally been provided an opportunity by the gods. All he had to do was win. And Ramaraya was going to do everything in his power to make it happen.

"Go, prepare the steam bath," Ramaraya commanded. Once Bisalappa left, Ramaraya continued to brood over Venkatadri's words.

"Why can't you understand, brother? A smaller army was always in the best interest of our Samrajya," he said. But as he said it, a small voice in the back of his head which had until now kept silent spoke.

That was not the only reason for reducing the power of the royal army now, Rama, was it?

******

# CHAPTER 6
# 1529

'Karnata Samrajya Chakravarti Achyutadevaraya had declared a month-long mourning for his departed brother, Krishnadevaraya. During this period, no house would cook any meals and all the people of the city would eat at the temples where a month-long puja had been organised in memory of Emperor Krishnadevaraya.'

The words were repeated by multiple criers throughout the streets of Samrajya.

"That should have been you, Anna," Tirumala said angrily looking out of the window to the street where people were gathered near a temple.

"He did not want me to succeed him," Ramaraya said, his voice trembling. "Why did he not want me to succeed him?"

"He made a mistake," Tirumala said turning his head back. They were gathered in Ramaraya's study room. Just him, his brothers and his wife, after having attended the last rites of Emperor Krishnadevaraya. Ramaraya did not know what hurt him more – the death of his father-in-law or the fact that Krishnadevaraya did not consider him worthy to be his successor.

"He chose Achyuta, who has been kept under house arrest for more than a decade over me. Why?" he asked looking at his wife.

Mohanagi drew to his side, her hands gently upon his brow.

"As Tirumala said, Swami, my father made a mistake," she said softly. "You are more qualified to sit on the throne compared to my uncle. Mother agrees with me as well."

"We still have time, brother. If we can convince enough Nayakas, then we can correct this mistake," Tirumala said.

"Can we?" Ramaraya asked as hope rose in his heart again.

"Mother will support us, Swami," Mohanagi nodded.

"Most of the Nayakas will support us, Anna," Tirumala added. "We can send messengers to most important Nayaka families to gain their support. I am confident they will support us versus Achyutaraya."

"It won't be enough, Anna," Venkatadri's voice came from the doorway. All heads turned towards him.

"What do you mean?" Tirumala demanded.

"I am coming from the royal barracks. The royal army has declared their allegiance to Achyutaraya," he said simply.

That felt like a hammer blow to Ramaraya as his momentary hope was swiftly crushed.

"What? Why?" Tirumala cried angrily.

"The soldiers said they would fulfil the last wishes of their beloved emperor."

"We can still ask for support from the Nayakas. We—"

"Let it go, Tirumala," Ramaraya said bitterly.

"But Anna..."

"We will go to the palace tomorrow and offer our support to the new emperor. For better or worst, Achyutaraya is the new emperor of Samrajya," Ramaraya declared, nearly choking on those words.

******

His reception at the palace was less than cordial. Achyutaraya sat on the royal throne flanked by his two brothers-in-law, Salakaraju

Chinna Tirumala and Salakaraju Peda Tirumala. Where Achyutaraya appeared uneasy in his new position, the two Salakarajus appeared like eagles waiting to pounce on anyone who might threaten their nascent power.

"Of all the Nayaka families, why did Emperor Krishnadevaraya marry his brother to their family?" Ramaraya cursed softly. But he knew that the Salakaraju family was the only other Nayaka family comparable to Aravidu family in influence and Krishnadevaraya hoping to pacify them, married his brother into their clan, assuming he would be succeeded by his son. Instead, his son's untimely death had brought the Salakarajus close to the power they so desperately desired.

"Mahaprabhu, please accept this jewel encrusted throne as a humble offering from your loyal servant," Ramaraya bowed as his servants brought forth an exquisite, gilded throne.

"It is very beautiful, Aravidu Ramaraya," the emperor declared. A servant brought a beeda on a tray.

"The Aravidu family have always served Samrajya loyally. As the head of your family, I ask you, Ramaraya, will you serve me with the same devotion that you once gave to my brother?"

"The Aravidu family will consider it as our honour," Ramaraya announced.

"Then come accept this sacred beeda as a symbol of your vow," he declared. Ramaraya approached the throne, bowed once more and cupped his hands forward. The emperor placed the beeda and Ramaraya raised it to his forehead. He paused briefly as he wrestled with the sadness and anger that had become his companions since the last few weeks. A small corner of his mind told him that he should refuse and instead seize the throne that belonged to him rightfully.

He did not want me to, the voice in his head reminded him as he placed the beeda in his mouth. Out of the corner of his eye, he saw a smile light up Salakaraju Chinna Tirumala's lips.

"We once again thank the Aravidu family and you for your loyalty," the emperor intoned.

Ramaraya nodded as he withdrew to where the rest of his kinsmen stood.

"I don't like this. That fool seems too pleased, Anna," Tirumala said, indicating Salakaraju Chinna Tirumala, who now wore an open grin.

"We will know soon enough," Ramaraya said calmly, even though he could fairly guess what the brothers had planned for him.

******

"They are exiling you, Anna; the nerve of those bastards," Tirumala exploded.

Ramaraya read the contents of the imperial letter one more time and smiled. "They waited till I took the oath publicly," he said appreciating the plot. He knew that it came from the mind of Salakaraju Chinna Tirumala. It was simple and brilliant at the same time.

"Who is being appointed as the governor of the Tamil lands?" Ramaraya asked.

"Chelappa," Tirumala replied.

"Of course, the one man who hates me more than even the Salakarajus," Ramaraya laughed.

"How can you be so casual about this, Anna?" Tirumala cried.

"Tirumala, you are getting needlessly worked up. I have appointed you as my Karyakarta; you will remain in the palace. The emperor will accept it, as he knows putting both of us under house arrest will not be taken lightly by our family. That said, I am rather looking forward to this role."

"Don't joke, Anna. Your official rank might be equal to Chelappa, but your authority does not extend beyond the city of Chandragiri and a few villages while he controls—"

"The entire wealth and men in the Tamil regions, I know," Ramaraya leaned back in his chair.

"That does not worry you?"

"No."

"Anna, they have even stripped your personal guards."

"That is not true, Tirumala. They have rewarded me for my service by exchanging my Rachebidas with the soldiers of the royal army," he said reading out a portion of the letter. "At least my jailers are going to be competent ones. It will give me a challenge."

Seeing Tirumala's incredulous expression, he laughed, "My dear brother, this is truly good news."

"Good, how?" Tirumala replied confused.

"Because I won't be here when things go wrong soon."

"Why would things go wrong?"

"Because by concentrating so much power in the hands of a single man, the emperor has made his first mistake."

"Chelappa is fanatically loyal to the emperor," Tirumala objected.

"Oh, he is...for now," Ramaraya placed his right leg on his left thigh to sit more comfortably. He closed his eyes and hummed softly.

"Anna, I don't understand."

"Neither does the emperor and that is what makes it so funny," Ramaraya hummed louder now.

*I hope you are watching this from the heavens, father-in-law, because I want you to observe the cost Samrajya pays for your decision,* he thought with some satisfaction.

******

## 1532

"Chelappa has led a revolt against the emperor," Tirumala announced barging into Ramaraya's study room where he was preparing to play the veena.

"That was quick," Ramaraya commented as he plucked the strings a few times. He frowned as it did not sound correct. He plucked it a few more times while adjusting the strings.

"Anna, the emperor has commanded the Aravidu troops to join Salakaraju Chinna Tirumala and the royal army to quell Chelappa's uprising."

"He wants you to lead our men?" Ramaraya asked.

"Venkatadri."

"Of course," Ramaraya grinned. "They feel our younger brother's almost complete devotion to military means he is more malleable compared to either of us."

"They are not wrong," Tirumala replied.

"Like I said Tirumala, I am just an observer and that is what I am going to do for now."

"Prabhu, may I enter?" Gunda, the commander of his 'guards' and his chief jailer asked.

"Come," Ramaraya invited him. Gunda's eyes fell on Tirumala, and he did not hide his displeasure. While they made all efforts to reduce Ramaraya's contact with the outside world, they could not deny Tirumala, his Karyakarta.

"If this is about Chelappa's rebellion, then I want you to tell the emperor that I am very troubled, and that the emperor has the full Aravidu army for him to command."

"He has already commanded your brother Venkatadri," Gunda said looking at Tirumala, as if wondering why he had not informed Ramaraya.

"That is a very good choice indeed," Ramaraya nodded.

"Prabhu, the emperor also wishes to inform you that he is reducing the number of men under you temporarily to five hundred cavalry. The rest will be sent to deal with the traitor."

"I understand," Ramaraya said pleasantly. "Are you going as well?" Ramaraya asked.

"I am, Prabhu," the man replied.

"Then I will pray to Virupaksha today that you and your men return safely."

"You are kind, Prabhu," Gunda bowed.

"Yes, I will actually pray to Lord Virupaksha to keep you and your men safe because you will die by my hands," Ramaraya swore once the man had left.

"Anna, do you think this is—"

"No, Tirumala," Ramaraya shook his head. "We are not going to talk of rebellion ever again," he said in a low tone. "You will continue to do what we have decided."

"Anna, Vishwanatha Nayaka has agreed to marry our cousin, but he wants fifteen war elephants as dowry."

"That man is certainly ambitious. He wants to emulate Lakkanna Dandesha and invade the island of Lanka," Ramaraya mused. "Very well, we will transfer the elephants from our army."

"But Anna, that will weaken our forces dangerously," Tirumala objected.

"We can get more elephants Tirumala, but a marital alliance with Vishwanatha Nayaka will boost our strength immensely. With him on our side, we will have tied all the major Nayaka families of Samrajya with our Aravidu family. Even the emperor will not risk offending us without a strong cause."

"Anna, I don't understand your objective. We have been building matrimonial alliances with the Nayaka families since the last two years. What purpose are these alliances if we don't intend to seize our rights?"

"The alliance will come in handy, Tirumala, at the opportune time," he said confidently. He plucked the strings again and gave a pleased sigh.

"Anna, how much longer do you think the emperor is going to keep you here?"

"Considering how his reign is progressing, it won't be for long," he predicted confidently.

"Perfect, it sounds perfect," he declared. "Sit Tirumala, I am playing a song by Purandaradasa. I want you to tell me what you think," he said playing the veena as he savoured the chaos that the emperor had reaped.

******

## 1534

The capital looked unchanged. Even after ruling for more than half a decade, Achyutaraya had not indulged in the same building spree as his brother.

Not surprising, considering he had spent most of his time tumbling from one disaster to the next. Although Ramaraya was not complaining as the emperor's blunders were the reason he was now in Vijayanagara.

He waited outside the royal court, waiting to be announced inside.

"Prabhu, you may go in," the guard at the door said with a bow. Ramaraya entered, walking towards the throne. The emperor was massaging his head gently. He raised his head at Ramaraya's approach.

Ramaraya was taken aback as he beheld the emperor's face, which seemed to have changed dramatically from the last time Ramaraya had seen him. For one, the emperor had aged by almost a decade. His hair had gone grey at multiple places. He looked emaciated and his teeth was bleached red, an effect of eating too much beeda.

"Mahaprabhu," Ramaraya bowed respectfully.

"Welcome Ramaraya, was your journey comfortable?" the emperor asked.

"The thought of being in your presence once more made me forget mundane things, Prabhu."

"Well said," a voice cried out from the crowd.

"Quiet!" the emperor declared. "Do you know why you are here?"

You want me to recover the prestige of Samrajya after you and your brothers-in-law have failed repeatedly against the Shahi kingdoms, he thought disgustedly.

"I am a simple servant of Samrajya, Mahaprabhu. I am here to carry out Mahaprabhu's wishes," he said aloud.

"Well said," cried more voices from the crowd. The emperor raised his hand for silence once again.

"Your dedication to Samrajya is truly commendable," Achyutaraya said. He waved forward a soldier who brought forth a jewel-encrusted sword and a beeda.

"During the days of my brother, the Shahis were scared to even venture out from their homes. Now they snap at our heels, targeting our border forts and villages. The worst offender is Qutb Shah. He has the temerity to capture even Warangal. The people of the place have begged me to free them from the oppressive rule of Qutb Shah and I have promised them that I'd save them. Ramaraya, I want you to be my sword and punish Qutb Shah for his crimes. Quench the hunger of my sword with Qutb Shah's blood."

Ramaraya picked up the sword.

"Mahaprabhu, I am honoured, and grateful for this opportunity," he said bowing deeply.

"I swear in the court that I will not return till I capture Warangal!" he declared to the shouts of approval of the crowd.

"Do this task for me and you may name your reward," the emperor announced.

"I am unworthy of the honour," Ramaraya declared bowing once again. Once more he saw the ghost of a smile on Salakaraju's lips. But this time he matched it with one of his own, causing Salakaraju's smile to falter.

******

"The royal army will not accompany us, save for a small troop," Tirumala said angrily.

"How else can they ensure that I too fail? Salakaraju Chinna Tirumala's repeated failures have made the emperor's position unstable."

"But without the royal army, our forces will be inadequate," Venkatadri said, ever the military man.

"I know," Ramaraya nodded.

"What do we do then, Anna?"

"We do what the emperor commanded. We ask for troops from the Nayakas," Ramaraya said.

"Even then we will not have enough men," Tirumala warned.

"We will, if all of the border Nayakas deploy their full strength," Ramaraya said confidently.

"They will never do that, Anna. They will not leave their territories undefended," Venkatadri shook his head.

"They will, for us. I think it is time to use those matrimonial alliances," Ramaraya said firmly.

"Anna, even then they will not deploy their entire forces," Venkatadri insisted.

"How much time do we have?" Ramaraya asked.

"The emperor has given us four months to prepare."

"That should be enough, Tirumala. Send forth your scribes. I need to dictate letters to all the Nayakas allied to us. They need to understand what is at stake," Ramaraya commanded as he read through the reports of their spies about the enemy military strength and preparations.

******

## 1535

"Did you have to give up all the loot?" Tirumala asked as the treasure inside the fort was brought before Ramaraya before being weighed and distributed among the junior commanders and soldiers.

"How did you guess that Qutb Shah would take the bait and attack Gajapatis? Anna," Venktadri asked in an awed voice.

"Because I knew he was the ultimate opportunist. I knew he would not lose the opportunity to raid Gajapati lands once he learned our forces were assaulting them from the south."

"But how did you know that he would retire to Warangal after attacking Gajapati lands."

"Warangal is the strongest fort that he possesses closest to Gajapati borders. Where else would he go?"

"Still, I expected him to put up a better fight," Venkatadri said, a bit disappointed.

"Qutb Shah did what all Shahis do when they want to conduct a swift campaign. He created his raiding force around his heavy cavalry supported by the garrisoned troops at the border forts."

It was a good strategy as it kept the supply lines small and kept the soldiers in the border garrisons satisfied. Unfortunately for Qutb Shah, Ramaraya planned to use the very propensity of raiding against him. A small Samrajya force raided Gajapati lands triggering the Gajapati armies to march south where they encountered the combined armies of the Nayakas ruling Andra lands. The Samrajya forces under the direction of Ramaraya did not fight the Gajapatis, rather they engaged them diplomatically and even surrendered wealth to soothe the tempers of the Gajapati ruler. The moment he heard of the Samrajya attack, Qutb Shah organised his own forces and launched a raid into Gajapati lands. It was at this moment that Ramaraya launched his own attack at Warangal, capturing the now weakened garrison easily.

"Anna, how will the emperor react to our attack on the Gajapati empire?"

"You mean the attack by robbers from Samrajya? I am sure Pemmasani Ramalinga has apologised for it by now," Ramaraya said innocently.

"What happens if Qutb Shah tries to retake Warangal?" Tirumala asked.

"He won't. He will have his hands full with the Gajapati armies, who are even now marching towards his lands to teach him a lesson," Ramaraya laughed.

"What will you ask the emperor as a reward?"

"I will ask for the honour of taking the emperor's nephew as my ward," Ramaraya replied.

"Sadashiva? He is a boy of two. Why do you want him?" Tirumala asked confused.

"Because I promised my wife," he lied.

# CHAPTER 7
# 1564

"Prabhu, I bring good news. Your brother, valiant Senapathi Tirumala Raya has managed to repulse the enemy assault on our fortification. The enemy fled shamelessly, leaving behind all their dead," the messenger exclaimed.

"How many dead?" Venkatadri demanded.

"Prabhu?" the messenger said looking confused.

"You said the enemy fled leaving behind their dead. How many of the enemy were killed?"

"I did not wait for the final tally, Prabhu. I was commanded by Senapathi Raghunatha to bring the news of the victory to you," the messenger told Ramaraya.

He had clearly ridden non-stop from the banks of Krishna as Venkatadri could see mud still sticking to his boots which he probably had cleaned in a hurry before the meeting.

I must not be hard on him. He is simply a messenger, Venkatadri told himself.

"Even a rough estimate would be good," he asked.

The messenger cleared his throat looking uncomfortable.

"Prabhu..."

"Were the enemy dead less than a hundred?"

"Maybe more," the messenger said weakly.

"You have done well," Ramaraya picked a small bag of coins that was kept within reach for such occasions. He threw the bag at the messenger who caught it and retreated from the room.

"We will need several hundred of such 'great' victories," Venkatadri declared.

"This is the boy's first actual fight. Have you forgotten yourself at the same age, Venkatadri?" Ramaraya asked sternly.

"Forgive me brother, but I cannot worry about feelings when Samrajya faces its gravest threat," Venkatadri replied standing up from his seat. They were alone in the room. Ramaraya had asked the messenger to report to them in the evening.

"Are you going to announce this to the assembly?" Venkatadri asked.

"Why not? Might be good for the morale," Ramaraya said.

"Anna, you know very well what is happening there. They are probing our defences, and our soldiers must have caught one of their scouting parties."

"Who strangely stood and fought," Ramaraya said thoughtfully. "Why?"

Venkatadri shook his head as he considered the fact as well.

"Seems like a waste of lives."

"And it's not the first time," Ramaraya said handing Venkatadri the palm leaf with the message from their brother Tirumala. He read it quickly,

"Seven," he exclaimed.

"Yes, if they are scouting then it's a rather strange way of doing it."

His brother was correct. Generally, scouts tended to avoid enemy forces and fortification, but here the Shahis seemed to be hitting the Samrajya forces all across the line.

"What do you suppose they are doing? I was expecting them to launch their expedition at the beginning of summer when the river level would be low enough to cross easily."

"That is the ideal time for campaigning," Venkatadri agreed. It was not simply because of the reduction in water levels of the rivers but also because that was the period of the year when the farmers would harvest their crops which was necessary to feed the army.

"Our spies have reported their main army is still camped near Bijapur," Ramaraya said.

"They can reach the river in less than a week," Venkatadri argued.

"We can reach it in less than ten days," Ramaraya said confidently.

"Anna, if they march with full strength then Tirumala won't be able to defend the forts," Venkatadri warned. Venkatadri watched his brother considering his words warily, worried that Ramaraya would disregard his concerns once again.

"We need at least another two months for the Nayakas from Tamil lands and the coast to reach Vijayanagara," Ramaraya said massaging his head weakly.

His brother's words triggered a sudden panic in Venkatadri's mind.

"Anna," he said, his chest heaving with concern.

"What?"

"That's it! That's what they are planning."

"What do you mean?"

"Anna, they know that if all our forces are concentrated, then they stand no chance."

"But if they can force the battle now, then they have a chance," Ramaraya nodded.

"Let me go, Anna. I will reinforce Tirumala," Venkatadri begged.

"No," Ramaraya shook his head.

"Anna—"

Ramaraya raised his hand to silence Venkatadri.

"Tirumala is commanding the force at the river as per my orders. If you take charge now, it will appear to him that I do not trust him."

"You cannot be serious, Anna," Venkatadri shivered as he tried to hold back his anger.

"I have made my decision, Venkatadri. You will prepare the army for the march, but will only march at my command," he ordered.

The command felt like a knife through him, and he was tempted to simply leave, abandoning his brother. But a corner of his mind reminded him what they were fighting for, so Venkatadri's only response was a sad nod. The only thought in his mind:

What if it was already too late?

******

Hussain Nizam was not pleased as the Adil Shahi soldier explained their progress or rather the lack of any in stopping the Samrajya armies from finishing their fortifications.

"You are telling me that they never gave chase to our fleeing men? Not even once?" Ibrahim Qutb Shah asked astonished.

"No, Huzoor, not even on the twentieth when they put us to flight."

"You fled leaving behind your dead?" Hussain Shah demanded.

"That is not the concern here," Ali interrupted. Hussain Shah glared at him and then at the messenger.

"That is the concern. If your men had pushed with their full strength, then god would have given us the victory," he said harshly.

"Your men were also part of the raiding force," Ibrahim Qutb Shah reminded him, which got him a disgusted look.

"They will be punished for the failure," he growled.

"Sultan, I think our priority must be to cross the Krishna river," Ali said.

"Do you think I do not understand?" Hussain Shah demanded angrily.

"If you do, then I suggest we march towards the river swiftly," Ali continued undaunted.

"The mercenaries..." Hussain Shah began.

"Will be able to catch up," Ibrahim Qutb Shah interjected.

Hussain Shah made a show of considering their words.

"Or we can march ahead while the Ahmednagar forces can stay here until the mercenaries arrive," Ali said innocently.

That earned him an even nastier glare from Hussain Shah.

"Nobody is going to rob me of the chance to take revenge on the Kaffir and his men," Hussain Shah declared.

"Then it is settled. We march in the morning. Prepare your men for a hard march," Ibrahim Qutb Shah told the gathered officers in the tent, irrespective of their allegiance.

Ali nodded, "We aim to reach within a week," he said.

"Let the enemy enjoy the last week of their life," Hussain Shah snorted.

That remains to be seen. Let us hope we are not too late, Ali thought grimly.

******

The armies marched like a many-headed snake, each of the heads was the cavalry force of a specific Shahi kingdom, riding separately. The infantry and elephants marched as a unified group.

"Huzoor, we should be able to see the enemy fortification in an hour," Kishwar Khan told Ali.

Ali nodded, taking advantage of the short pause to pull out his water skin and throw some water on to his face to cool himself. The midday sun was mercilessly beating down upon them, but Ali was still satisfied. They had made here in just four days.

"Well, at least the cavalry," he corrected himself. But the combined Shahi cavalry was still a formidable force capable of seizing a foothold easily.

He spied a horseman coming from the east. He spent a few moments trying to identify him as the man's armour was caked in mud.

"It's one of Hussain Shah's messengers," Kishwar Khan said.

"Let him approach me," Ali said.

The messenger got down from his horse and prostrated before Ali.

"Just get on with delivering the message," Ali said irritably as the man tried to follow up with a formal salute.

"Huzoor, my master, the most valiant hero of the faith has told me to inform you to hurry to his position. He wants you to be a witness as he and his warriors scatter the enemy at the river."

"Has he done the reconnaissance? What's the strength of the enemy at that location?" Ali demanded.

"Huzoor, the faithful—"

"Ride now and do not stop till you reach your master's position," he commanded the messenger. The man stood his mouth hanging open.

"*Now!*" Ali screamed. The man turned his horse and rode back.

"We follow him immediately Kishwar Khan before Hussain Shah gets all his men killed!" he screamed whipping his horse viciously as they tore after the messenger.

******

The sound of fighting reached Ali's ears even over the sound of his galloping horses. As they neared, they could see things clearer now. The river was already red with blood of men and horses. Across the river a fierce fight was being waged for the possession of the wooden fort that had been built at a crossing. It was not the only fort as Ali saw that the Samrajya forces had built multiple such forts as far as his eye could see, at places where there was a crossing.

"Maybe they have spread themselves thin," he hoped as more of Hussain Shah's men plunged their horses into the raging river. Many men and their horses were swept away. The others were attacked with arrows and muskets. The 'lucky' one who reached the fort walls scrambled up using scaling ropes to overwhelm the defenders.

"Surely there are easier ways of dismissing unwanted mercenaries," Kishwar Khan commented watching the battle. Ali watched helplessly as another group of Ahmednagar cavalry rode in as reinforcements.

He turned his head and located Hussain Shah screaming at his commanders.

"Why doesn't he lead the next lot himself?" Ali asked unkindly. But he turned back to the river as the cavalrymen bravely charged into the river after their comrades.

"They might make it," Kishwar Khan said excitedly.

"I think not," Ali sighed pointing across the river where a large body of enemy cavalry were now riding to the aid of the defenders. The enemy cavalry split into two groups, the first one rode to the fort and second group moved to intercept the Hussain Shah cavalrymen who had managed to cross the river and were trying to regroup. The Samrajya cavalry fell upon them, swiftly scattering them with a fierce charge.

That left the men scaling the fort who now faced the dismounted heavy Samrajya cavalrymen. Here too the result was the same as Hussain Shah's men were routed quickly.

"I hope he has learned something today," Kishwar Khan said.

"I doubt it," Ali shook his head as Hussain Shah continued to berate his men.

******

Ali headed to Hussain Shah's tent later in the evening, fully planning to give him a piece of his mind. But as he neared the camps of the Ahmednagar army, he heard the screams of men in great pain. The entire camp appeared to have gone deathly quiet, save for the moaning. Once Hussain Shah's tent became visible, Ali saw the source of the moaning. Arranged in two lines facing one another were men, stripped till the waist. They were tied to wooden pillars as tall as a man. Each man had been flogged to within an inch of his lines. They were bleeding profusely, the blood forming pools underneath their feet. Ali looked at Kishwar Khan who too struggled to hide his distaste.

"Cut them down!" came a harsh command. Ali turned and saw Ibrahim Qutb Shah had come up with his officers. A single soldier standing guard near the condemned men ran up to them.

"Huzoor, the Sultan has commanded that they remain like this till morning as a punishment for fleeing the battle."

"Cut them down," Ibrahim said coldly, waving his own men forward to obey his command.

Ali and Ibrahim shared a silent look as if having similar thoughts.

"We will have to try again tomorrow," Ali said.

"With better co-ordination than today," Ibrahim nodded.

"How will we convince him?" Ali asked.

"He will see reason, or he can watch me return to Golconda with my men tomorrow morning," Ibrahim said coldly.

"That is pretty much what I was thinking," Ali said with equal savagery.

"Good, then let us have another chat with father-in-law," Ibrahim said with a humourless grin, opening the tent flap and entering inside without waiting for the servant to announce him.

Ali followed with a satisfied grin.

******

The Bijapur soldiers charged at the fort in three waves, with infantry archers leading the assault. The archers sent a barrage of arrows at the fort aiming to keep the enemy pinned down as the second wave composed of light infantry plunged into the raging waters to wade across to the other side. Once across, they were instructed to attack the fort from the landward side. While that occupied the enemy attention, the heavy dismounted Bijapur cavalry would approach the fortress walls using small boats and attack the defenders. It was as good a plan as Ali could come up with in the short time, but even then, Ali knew there was a possibility that the assault might fail.

"No matter, one of us would succeed," Ali muttered thinking of the similar assaults being launched by Ibrahim Qutb Shah and Hussain Nizam Shah's men at two other places. It was hoped one of them would succeed, giving the allies the control of one of the forts.

The archers appeared to be succeeding as the enemy return volley was weak and uncoordinated. Ali signalled for the second wave and watched his men rush to the waters. They were bare-chested; their weapons and shields tied to their back with thick ropes. Many more followed with extremely large turbans made from strong rope which would be used as scaling ropes once they reached their destination. Ali gripped the reins of his horse tightly, praying for his men as they plunged into the waters. A few were swept away, while some were hit by arrows fired by the defenders. But most managed to cross the river.

"They have done it!" Kishwar Khan exclaimed excitedly.

The third wave composed of the elite cavalrymen that now approached their boats.

"Huzoor?" Kishwar Khan asked. The infantrymen who had crossed quickly formed ranks and then started their assault.

Ali signalled for the cavalry to begin their assault. The cavalrymen in their heavy armour climbed the boats which wobbled under the weight of the armoured warriors.

"Send a message to Amir Afzal not to overload the boats. Let the boatman decide how many men their boats can take," Ali ordered. As the messenger rode carrying his command, one of the boats sank into the river under the weight of the men, the men struggling wildly to save themselves. But under the weight of their armour, most of them sank like stones. Luckily for them as they were still near the shore, they were saved by the infantrymen.

As if learning from that experience, the remaining boats reduced their numbers before heading to the enemy fort. Until now, everything seemed to be going according to their plan. Which strangely made Ali worried.

"Why are they not defending the fort better?" he wondered.

Then a few moments later, as though the enemy had heard his thoughts, a rocket was launched from inside the fort into the sky. And immediately like a sleeping elephant that had been woken up, the fortress walls were filled with archers who attacked with vengeance. Ali's archers, who had been shooting for nearly half an hour, tried to respond, but they were outnumbered. The enemy focussed on the boats, shooting the defenceless cavalrymen in the boats. To add to it, Ali heard horses in the distance and saw a large body of enemy cavalry riding to the fortress, their targets the infantrymen who were assaulting the fort and were in the open.

"They predicated our moves," Kishwar Khan said in a quiet voice.

"Yes," Ali said not hiding his bitterness. "We squandered our chance by launching a pre-emptive attack yesterday."

"Maybe the others might have had better success," Kishwar Khan said trying to sound positive.

"I doubt it," Ali shook his head. "Order a withdrawal. We have lost enough men for the day."

"Huzoor," Kishwar Khan bowed. Ali could see the disappointed look on the faces of his officers.

"This is merely a setback," he said cooly. "We will have to change our tactics."

"Huzoor, should we request for another meeting with the other sultans?" Kishwar Khan asked.

"No, I have a plan," Ali said confidently.

******

Ali found the man sitting in his tent, looking a bit uncomfortable.

"Huzoor," the man stood up bowing respectfully.

"What did you think of the assault?" Ali asked.

"A lot of effort for very little gain, Huzoor," the man replied. Then as if shocked by his bashfulness he quickly hesitated, "I meant, Huzoor..."

Ali waved his hand dismissively, "I am not offended by honesty, Parashuram," Ali replied. "Do you know why you are here?" he asked.

Parashuram shook his head.

"When I offered a chance for your people to serve Bijapur Sultan, many of my Amirs said you people are too unruly and weak to be of any use to me."

"Huzoor, you only have to command us," Parashuram declared.

"Parashuram, I believe that you and your men will be of great use to Bijapur. You can go where my regular army cannot, succeed in situations where pure military strength is not enough. I need your skill and your light cavalry."

"We are yours to command, Huzoor," Parashuram bowed.

"Find me a way across," Ali commanded.

"Huzoor, how many days do we have?"

"No more than a fortnight," Ali said.

"It will be done, Huzoor," Parashuram promised and left without another word. Ali sat back in his chair with a sigh, wondering how the enemy would take the news of this failed assault.

******

# CHAPTER 8
# 1543

He had failed them all – his family, the people of Samrajya and most importantly, the one man whom Ramaraya had truly admired and respected.

"If Mahaprabhu Krishnadevaraya was here, this would not have happened," a Nayaka cavalryman muttered from behind. Ramaraya turned his back glaring at the man who flinched visibly seeing Ramaraya's fury.

Ramaraya fought to regain his temper, "Not now," he told himself, but promised that the man would not see tomorrow's sun.

"What shall we do, Anna?" his brother Venkatadri asked. Ramaraya thought he saw tears in his brother's eyes, but Venkatadri quickly blinked it away. Ramaraya knew Venkatadri was not the only man among his force who was affected by the sight that greeted them when they reached Vijayanagara after defeating the forces of the traitor Salakaraju Tirumala.

Vijayanagara, the crown jewel of the Samrajya was burning.

"Is this his attempt at extracting a final revenge upon us and the Samrajya?" Venkatadri said watching the flames rising higher now.

"If we ride hard, we could be inside the city within a couple of hours. Then we can help the Kavalagaras to save our city," a soldier cried.

Ramaraya did not respond, but his eyes went to the north, where a large army was camped upon the plains in front of the city, the men watching the fire of Vijayanagara with ill-concealed happiness. Ibrahim Adil Shah's army had arrived as arbitrators between the loyal armies of Samrajya, led by Ramaraya and the traitors under the command of Salakaraju Tirumala. Salakaraju Tirumala was appointed as the guardian of his nephew, a boy of six, Venkata, upon the death of his father, emperor Achyutaraya. It was done at the insistence of the queen as she probably hoped that they would be safest under the guardianship of her younger brother. The arrangement lasted less than six months, ending with the murders of the queen and her infant son. He then followed it up with whole massacre of anyone even remotely associated with the Tuluva dynasty. It was probably his attempt at establishing a new dynasty with him at its head, but he missed one Tuluva scion, Sadashiva Raya who was still under the care of Ramaraya.

It was the opportunity that Ramaraya was awaiting since the death of Krishnadevaraya. When he learnt of Salakaraju's treachery, he led a massive coalition army to punish Salakaraju Chinna Tirumala. The traitor soon discovered that he was isolated with almost all the Nayakas of the empire siding with Ramaraya. Desperation caused Salakaraju to invite Adil Shah to his aid, paid by the vast treasury of Samrajya that successive emperors had accumulated.

They had come, although the civil war was a purely internal matter of Samrajya. Ibrahim Adil Shah had ignored propriety for gold that Salakaraju had offered, an offer that Ramaraya had been forced to exceed to rid the enemy army from the Samrajya lands. But even after getting paid twice and doing absolutely nothing, Ibrahim Adil Shah was content to sit in front of Vijayanagara watching it burn while daring Ramaraya to enter the city in the presence of a hostile army.

"Bastard," Ramaraya growled glaring at the enemy army.

"Prabhu, what shall we do?" Bisalappa, the commander of his cavalry enquired, his voice calm.

Ramaraya could feel all their eyes upon him, waiting for his decision.

What would you have done, *Mava*? Ramaraya wondered thinking about Krishnadevaraya, but he knew the answer even before he asked.

"Send a messenger to my brother Tirumala, ask him to hurry with the main body of cavalry. I want him here before nightfall," he commanded.

"And us?" Venkatadri asked.

"We are going to enter the city and save the people," he said loudly.

"What about the army of Ibrahim Adil Shah?" Venkatadri asked.

"He better be ready to fight to stop me because I have no intention of failing the Samrajya today," Ramaraya cried. His men screamed their approval as he led his forces in a charge towards the city main gates.

******

"Prabhu, haven't you done enough? The fires are put out," Bisalappa almost begged. Ramaraya did not hear the man at first as he helped a few Kavalagaras to move a half-burnt pillar that had been the part of the royal palace only a few hours earlier.

"Anna," Tirumala urged, pulling Ramaraya's arm.

Ramaraya glared his brother, "What?" he demanded harshly.

"You have saved the city, Anna; the damage has been restricted to the royal compound because of our efforts. You are a hero."

Ramaraya looked down at his hands which were covered in soot as were his clothes, "I don't feel like it," he said angrily.

"Feel like what?" Tirumala asked.

"A hero. I don't feel like I am one," Ramaraya replied. "*I* let the traitor seize power, *I* let him amass an army and *I* failed to stop him extracting his posthumous vengeance on Vijayanagara. Me, Tirumala. I have failed in my promise that I gave to emperor Krishnadevaraya upon his deathbed. I could not protect the Samrajya."

"Anna, there is no point in thinking of the past. If the emperor had named you his successor, none of this would have happened," Tirumala said in a low voice.

"We have discussed it Tirumala, the emperor did not trust my ability to lead the Samrajya and considering what happened, I feel he might have been right."

"You cannot blame yourself for this. If Emperor Achyutaraya had not trusted that traitor Salakaraju and given him the command of the royal army, all of this could have been avoided."

Ramaraya wanted to believe his brother's words. It was true in that Krishnadevaraya's successor, Achyutaraya had side-lined Ramaraya, fearing Ramaraya's power and influence. He had instead placed his trust in his brother-in-law Salakaraju Tirumala. The events after Achyutaraya's death had proved that his trust had been misplaced, but Ramaraya could not find any solace in that knowledge. He saw the people of the city looking at him in anger, a silent accusation in their eyes. Krishnadevaraya had entrusted Ramaraya with a duty – to protect the Samrajya and the Tuluva family. He had failed on both his tasks. Now he was at a loss – what to do next, how to regain his honour.

"Anna, Ibrahim Adil Shah has finally withdrawn," Venkatadri said coming up to him.

"His baggage trains are full of our wealth," Tirumala growled.

"If he was not here, we could have prevented Salakaraju from carrying out so much destruction."

"Yet he was here, as were contingents of the other Shahi kingdoms. They are the children of Bahmani empire and as such they think it's their right to interfere in the internal affairs of Samrajya," Ramaraya growled more to himself than anyone else.

"What shall we do now, Anna?" Tirumala asked.

"Do?" Ramaraya looked at him, "What else? We must crown Sadashiva as the new emperor."

"Anna, perhaps..." Tirumala began.

"No," Ramaraya said harshly. "Venkatadri, prepare for the coronation."

******

With the royal assembly badly burnt, the coronation ceremony of Sadashivaraya was held at the Virupaksha temple. It was fitting, Ramaraya decided, as once at this very place where Harihara Raya was crowned as the first emperor of the Samrajya, ending the dark period of death and destruction for the people at the hands of foreign invaders. Today, once more, an emperor would be crowned at this sacred place, at a time when the trust of the people in the Samrajya was at an all-time low. The emperor was little more than a boy, mere eight years. And he treated the ceremony like a game as he clapped happily as the priests chanted the sacred hymns. Ramaraya watched many of the Nayakas regarding their new emperor with avaricious looks as they hoped to gain advantages for themselves.

"Not till I am around," Ramaraya thought angrily. The Rajaguru, Tathacharya placed the crown over Sadashiva's head.

"Karnata Samrajya, Chakravati, Maharaja Sadashivaraya," chanted Tathacharya.

"Maharaja Sadashivaraya," Ramaraya cried out loudly along with everyone assembled.

Sadashiva looked at Ramaraya and he gave the boy an encouraging smile. He looked at Tathacharya, who raised his hand asking for silence. He then beckoned Ramaraya.

"Due to the young age of our emperor, the council and the dowager queens of the great Emperor Krishnadevaraya have decided to appoint Ramaraya as the regent of the empire."

There was a shocked silence at the announcement, but Ramaraya approached the throne kneeling before the emperor. Tathacharya handed him a sword and seal, which the boy placed into Ramaraya's hands.

"With this I trust the safety and future of our Samrajya into your hands," he said in a small voice. He had even managed to get the words across without a single mistake. Ramaraya looked at the boy and smiled almost paternally at his ward.

"May Virupaksha grant me the strength to fulfil my duties," he said loudly.

"You are the best man of the job, *Mava*," emperor Sadashiva declared.

"I will always strive to uphold Mahaprabhu's trust in me," Ramaraya responded. He turned to regard the crowd, which still appeared to be digesting the news of Ramaraya's sudden elevation to a position only a single step beneath the emperor. He knew there would be opposition and his eyes scanned the hall, mentally noting the names of the Nayakas who might challenge him in the future. He would deal with them in due time, but not today. Today Ramaraya was not worried, for he finally had managed to put himself in a position to save the Samrajya.

******

"Anna, I don't understand. That should have been you on that throne today," Tirumala said once the ceremony was completed. The three brothers were walking inside the temple compound, maintaining a respectful distance.

"Don't talk sacrilege, Anna," Venkatadri snapped angrily. It was a topic that caused many an argument among the two. Tirumala wanted Ramaraya to seize the throne, just as Saluva family overthrew the Sangama family before they themselves were overthrown by the Tuluva family. Now, Tirumala felt it was the time of their own family, the Aravidu, to take over the throne. But Venkatadri disagreed. His loyalty to the Tuluva family and to the memory of Krishnadevarya absolute. Ramaraya saw Tirumala preparing to respond, but he shook his head gently.

"I have made my decision," he said gently. Tirumala looked clearly disappointed by that response, but he did not speak further.

"The emperor is safely on the throne, but the empire is still unstable. There are many Nayakas who think this is perfect time to assert their independence. The Shahis will soon be back at our borders, raiding our lands. The destroyed portions of the city must be rebuilt and finally we must bring the same peace and prosperity that our people enjoyed during the time of the great Krishnadevaraya."

"That is going to take us many years, Anna," Venkatadri said with a loud sigh.

"Then I suggest we start immediately; Tirumala, send messages to the Nayakas, reminding of their fealty towards the emperor. Venkatadri, make sure the army is ready in case we might have to convince them of their duty," Ramaraya commanded.

His brothers bowed respectfully and departed along with their guards. Ramaraya watched them leave for a few seconds, turning his head back towards the temple pond, the Pushkarani. The cool wind was blowing as the day quickly turned to night and Ramaraya stood silently, watching the tiny waves of water in the pond. His mind wrestling with emotions that wracked him every day since that day when Emperor Krishnadevaraya had declared Achyutaraya as the emperor instead of him, Ramaraya.

You did not trust me, father-in-law. To protect and nourish the Samrajya, like you had done, he thought bitterly. I would have been the best choice to lead our people. Surely even you could have seen that and yet you did not name me your heir. Instead, you made me swear an oath to act as an eternal servant of the throne. To see useless and incompetent men ascend the throne in my stead.

Ramaraya took a deep breath, trying to master his mind as the feeling of betrayal and anger threatened to overwhelm him.

Very well Mava, I will not take the throne, but I will prove to you and everyone in the Samrajya that I am the greatest ruler of Samrajya, greater than even yourself.

******

# CHAPTER 9
# 1565

The news of the failed attacks did not improve Venkatadri's mood. Instead, his anxiety increased considerably. Tirumala and Raghunatha had done admirably, even brilliantly, to block the enemy advance, but the enemy would find a way to cross Krishna; of that Venkatadri was certain.

I should have been there, Venkatadri thought clenching his fist in frustration. He briefly considered speaking to his brother once more but dismissed it as futile. His brother still seemed to consider the Shahi threat as a minor annoyance.

"Prabhu," one of the guards entered the tent.

"What is it?" Venkatadri asked.

"Hande Hanumappa Nayaka is here," the guard said.

Venkatadri's face lit up at the news, "Send him in," he commanded.

Hande Hanumappa was a strongly built man, just a few years younger than Venkatadri. He looked tired, his face streaked with sweat and mud.

"Did you ride non-stop?" Venkatadri asked gripping his friend's outstretched hand.

"Originally I had not, but I heard the news of the failed assaults," Hanumappa said, a puzzled expression on his face. "Why are we still here, Mahasenapathi?" he asked simply.

"Because we are still waiting for our reserves to arrive from interior of the empire," Venkatadri said, giving the 'official' reason.

Hanumappa Nayaka gave a snort, "And the unofficial reason?"

"Anna is not convinced."

"Of the intentions of the enemy to destroy Samrajya?" Hanumappa Nayaka asked surprised.

"That he is certain of, but he still doubts their ability to do it," Venkatadri sighed.

"So, our mad dash here was for nothing," Hanumappa grunted.

"If it makes you feel any better, I for one am glad that you are here. I spent that last several months discussing with men who are either too young to understand what we face or are too old to care."

"We are no spring bucks ourselves," Hanumappa responded.

"We are not," Venkatadri nodded painfully as his familiar fear returned.

"Sadashiva Nayaka?"

"He does not have much time left in this world. If he was here then he would have advocated a direct attack on the Shahis on multiple fronts to pre-empt them," Venkatadri laughed.

"That he would have," Hanumappa agreed. "What about his son?"

"He injured himself a month back. Broke his leg during hunting. He sent his cousin with his soldiers."

"We don't need soldiers. We need capable commanders," Hanumappa sighed.

"Yes, we do, and we kept ignoring the problem for decades."

"It was not bad before, we still had a few capable commanders."

"Moulded in the fires of the campaigns under Emperor Krishnadevaraya."

"That leaves us with a serious problem. The enemy possess a good number of capable commanders."

"We cannot fail Samrajya, Hanumappa," Venkatadri.

"We won't," his friend promised.

******

Ali watched another half-hearted attempt at crossing the river fail, costing them several hundred men.

"Huzoor, we cannot keep this up infinitely," Kishwar Khan warned.

"Any news from Parashuram and his men?"

"No Huzoor," Kishwar Khan did not hide his distaste.

"You doubt them?"

"Huzoor, our glorious warriors have failed to break through the enemy. I fail to see how a bunch of mounted farmers will do any better."

"We will see."

"Huzoor, if I may ask something?" Kishwar Khan hesitated.

Ali smiled knowing what question his most loyal commander was going to ask.

"Why trust them in such an important task, Huzoor. They are not..."

"Equal to our soldiers because they believe in the same gods as Samrajya?" Ali finished his words.

"Yes, I know what we have been taught, Kishwar, but tell me this – how many times has our army managed to reach Vijayanagara?"

"Once under your father," Kishnwar Khan said instantly.

"How many times have they reached Bijapur?" he could see Kishwar Khan hesitate.

"Multiple times," Ali finished for him.

"But under the Bahmani Sultans, our armies have attacked Vijayanagara multiple times," Kishwar Khan said proudly.

"Yes, it was also the Bahmani empire that had to shift its capital from Gulbarga to Bidar. If we are invincible, then why did we have to do it?”

Again, Kishwar Khan looked away.

“If wars could be won based on the words of the poets, then the countries with the best poets would win. The reason I trust Parashuram and his men to accomplish this mission is because they, unlike our soldiers, have a lot to lose. This opportunity represents to them a chance to significantly improve the lives of his people. Parashuram understands it better than everyone. That is why I am confident he and his men will succeed.” Ali said simply.

Kishwar Khan was about to say something further when a soldier came running carting a pigeon.

“Huzoor, as per your command, I have this messenger pigeon from Parashuram.”

Ali waited for the soldier to remove the message scroll. He scrolled it open and read the terse message, a smile lighting his face.

‘Prepare an assault force, Kishwar Khan. We are just at the location of a new target.’

******

“Bisalappa, prepare a force of two thousand Rachebidas.”

“Odeya,” Bisalappa bowed.

“Virappa, you will lead them to my brother,” he told the second man who stood in the chamber. The two men bowed and departed.

“Swami, I feel we should send the remaining army at the capital to aid your brother, Tirumala,” Mohanagi told him once they had left. She was gently massaging his aching forehead. He squirmed as her fingers pressed a spot where the ache was rather fierce.

“Swami, I have told you many times to stop taking all the responsibilities yourself. You must let others do some work as well,” she chided him.

Ramaraya smiled lovingly at her, “Well, how else can I get my wife to massage me?” he asked playfully.

“I am serious, Swami,” she said as she rubbed a little bit more of the pain-relieving oil on her fingers and continued to massage him.

“Why else am I not sending Venkatadri? I do not want Tirumala to feel that I do not trust him.”

“But Swami, you must realise that Tirumala will be overwhelmed by the sheer number of the enemy. How much longer can he continue to hold them at bay?”

It was a thought that Ramaraya often had, but he was concerned that if he sent Venkatadri now and if he failed to reach Tirumala before the enemy crossed the river, then the enemy would face two divided Samrajya armies instead of a single large host.

“Better that we wait for the reinforcements from interior and assemble a grand army,” he told himself once again. But that plan was looking increasingly precarious as the reinforcements were still more than a month away.

“Swami,” Mohanagi gently placed her hand on his cheek.

“What?” Ramaraya asked.

“I asked, can’t you send Venkatadri and his army to Mudgal fortress? They will be close to Tirumala to provide aid if required, but at the same time it won’t look like you are interfering in Tirumala’s command.”

Ramaraya held Mohanagi at her shoulders.

“That is a very good plan,” he said happily. “If Venkatadri and his army is stationed at Mudgal, then the enemy, even if they cross the river will be forced to siege it as they cannot afford to leave such a large fortress in their rear before marching to Vijayanagara.”

“You can lead the reinforcements from the coast and Tamil lands yourself later,” Mohanagi added.

"Yes, that is what I will do," Ramaraya declared happily.

******

"Where are they going?" Venkatadri demanded loudly as a large force of Rachebidas rode through the city and towards the gates. Seeing the bewildered faces of his guards, Venkatadri resolved to find out himself. He quickly changed and had just started with his breakfast when a messenger arrived from his brother.

"Prabhu, Sarvadhikari Ramaraya has sent for you," the messenger said in a formal tone.

Now what? Venkatadri wondered as he gulped his meal swiftly before riding to the palace. The messenger led him to Ramaraya's private audience chambers and Venkatadri was surprised to find Hande Hanumappa already present, along with other senior commanders.

"I hope nothing has happened," Venkatadri muttered as he tried not to link the Rachebidas' sudden departure to this meeting.

Ramaraya came in after some time. He wore a simple silk dhoti and a necklace of prayer beads. His brother had come immediately after his morning prayers.

"Mahasenapathi, how soon can the army march?" he asked Venkatadri in a formal tone.

"Prabhu, as per your command, I have kept the men ready for departure at a moment's notice. We can march today or if Prabhu allows, tomorrow morning, which will give us time to obtain any last-minute supplies for the army," he responded equally formally.

"Tomorrow morning will be fine. You will march with haste and garrison Mudgal."

"Mudgal, Prabhu?" Venkatadri asked.

"Yes, you will be close enough to aid Tirumala, if he requires it,"

Ramaraya said. The words relieved Venkatadri as that meant the enemy were still on the opposite banks of Krishna.

"Prabhu, I saw a large body of Rachebidas heading north," Hanumappa said.

"I sent them to aid my brother. They will be able to provide him with a powerful counter in case the enemies manage to gain initiative," Ramaraya said.

Venkatadri and Hanumappa nodded appreciatively.

"How long will you take to reach Mudgal?"

"A week at most," Venkatadri said confidently.

"Go then, I will follow once all the reinforcements have arrived," Ramaraya declared.

Venkatadri bowed respectfully and turned to leave.

"Stay brother," Ramaraya commanded.

"What made you change your mind, brother?" Venkatadri asked once the others had departed.

"I haven't. Tirumala is still the commander of the Samrajya armies, tasked with stopping the enemy from crossing the river. You will provide him with aid only if he asks," Ramaraya said sternly.

"I will obey, Anna," Venkatadri said stiffly.

"I did not want our armies too far apart if the enemy actually manages to cross the river," Ramaraya said.

"Anna, if the enemy crosses the river, then I will engage them and defeat them. This I promise," Venkatadri swore.

"I know you will brother, and I will be there, watching you do it," Ramaraya said with a broad smile.

"Anna, you..."

"We will have no other discussion about this, Venkatadri. If the enemy crosses the river, then we will fight them, with or without our remaining army."

"As you say, Prabhu," Venkatadri said. Ramaraya came to him and embraced him tightly.

"Be careful, brother. I will not lose you to this stupid war. Do not do anything rash till I get there," he commanded.

******

Ali led a large force under the plain view of the enemy towards one of the forts, as if intending to cross. He saw the enemy had already started to prepare their own men to repulse Ali's forces, confident in the outcome.

"Not this time," Ali promised. He signalled his men to launch their attack. A dozen cannons fired simultaneously, signalling the start of the attack. Ali tracked the path of the projectiles, which landed all around the fort, but not even one hit the walls.

"It was too much to accept," Ali sighed. The cannons were splendid weapons, but they had their limitations, the chief one being their extremely poor accuracy. He watched the gunners dab the cannons with water to cool them to be able to fire once again. That would take several minutes, so Ali turned back to the assault which was led by the light infantry who swam through the waters to attack the fort from the landward side. A large body of cavalry were now mounting the rafts to begin the amphibious attack. To the Samrajya soldiers on the fort, it must appear like Ali was too stupid to try anything other than a direct assault.

Ali grinned as the enemy reacted exactly how they had done earlier. The soldiers on the walls engaged Ali's amphibious attackers while a rocket was launched to let the cavalry stationed in the rear to ride to the rescue of the fort defenders.

Only moments later they could hear a large force of cavalry charging towards the fort. A cheer went through the fort as the enemy soldiers redoubled their efforts to defend against the amphibious assault; the land attack left to the reinforcing cavalry.

"They have taken a lot of casualties," Ali commented.

"Or they could not liberate enough enemy uniforms," Kishwar Khan said.

Ali smiled as the cavalry reached the walls. A few even approached the gates, demanding to be let inside. Ali held his breath as he watched the exchange between the fortress defenders and the cavalry.

"Will they buy it?" Ali wondered. Then the enemy gate sung inwards to let the cavalry inside. Ali let his breath slowly as more and more cavalrymen entered the fort.

"Send in all the rafts," Ali commanded. The enemy arrow volley lowered in intensity and then stopped completely. The only sound was that of fierce fighting inside the fort. More of Ali's warriors landed on the opposite shore adding to their numbers.

"Kishwar Khan, we have only a small window before Tirumala and his son realises that we have seized the fort. I want our heavy cavalry and cannons across first. We must defend against a counterattack. Send a message to Ibrahim to bring his men here."

"What about Hussain Shah?"

"I am tempted to let him lose more of his men, but no, we will need every soldier in the coming fight. Send a message to him as well. Tell him the warriors of Bijapur have captured the enemy fort. Our path towards Vijayanagara is now unopposed."

******

It took Tirumala more than a day to realise that the Shahis had seized one of the forts. By then, most of Ali's forces and a large portion of Hussain Shah's men had crossed. Ibrahim Qutb Shah's armies were still waiting for a chance to cross the river. But the enemy was not about to let the Shahis cross unimpeded. As he watched, a large Samrajya force advanced against their position. There was no attempt at forming any battle order; instead the sound of trumpets indicated that Tirumala had ordered for a general assault. The enemy force charged towards the Shahi positions. Leading them were a large body of heavy armoured soldiers, dressed in blood red armour. Ali recognised them instantly – Ramaraya's personal guards, the Rachebidas.

"Kishwar Khan, order our cannons to fire at the appropriate range. Deploy the archers, I want them to thin out the enemy. You take command of the cavalry, I don't—" he stopped as a sound of trumpets and war cries erupted from their own ranks. Ali watched incredulously as a large body of Nizam Shahi cavalry charged towards the enemy.

"What is that fool doing?" Ali cried worried. His gunners looked at him helplessly as their shots were now blocked by Hussain Shah's men. The two forces smashed into each other, claiming the lives of dozens of men and horses. A fierce melee was waged, the Rachebidas cutting down Hussain Shah's men like a farmer in a rice field.

"Should we send our men?" Kishwar Khan asked.

"So that they too can be slaughtered?" Ali growled. Hussain Shah's forces were being pushed back and Ali urged them to retreat swifter so that his gunners could get a shot at the enemy.

"Come on," he urged uselessly. Then suddenly, a cannon boomed from their lines, landing among the enemies.

"Who fired that?" Ali demanded angrily at his gunners, but they looked as surprised as him. Then another shot was fired, followed by another. Ali could now see the source of the cannons. Hussain Shah's army.

"Their own men are among the enemy," Kishwar Khan said.

"He knows, but does not care," Ali said not trying to hide his distaste. "He sent them to slow the enemy while his gunners set up."

"But why sacrifice his men?" Kishwar Khan asked looking horrified.

Ali shrugged, "Order our men to fire as well. If Hussain Shah does not care for his men, I fail to see why should I?" he said grimly.

******

Rumi Khan turned his head to towards Hussain Shah once more, hoping that he would order him to cease fire. But Hussain Shah seemed to be entirely engrossed in watching the death and destruction.

"They are your own men," Rumi Khan whispered bitterly. Unfortunately, he knew that it was not entirely accurate; the cavalrymen that Hussain Shah had decided to sacrifice were mercenaries, like Rumi Khan and his men. The reason they were chosen for this dubious honour was because they dared to demand payment in gold from Hussain Shah.

I told Tahir not to threaten to leave Hussain Shah's service, Rumi Khan thought but Tahir had not listened to him. Hussain Shah was sending multiple messages with this action today.

Rumi Khan turned back towards his guns as his men were working hard to prepare the cannons for another volley. The enemy cavalry continued to advance, led by the cavalrymen in red armour. Even point-blank volley by Adil Shahi cannons were insufficient to stop them. It appeared as if the enemy would reach their lines soon.

"Huzoor, we are ready for another volley," cried one of his gunners. Rumi Khan ran down taking command of one of the guns.

"Aim your gun there," he indicated to a clump of horse led by a man who looked like the leader of the elite cavalrymen.

The man saw Rumi Khan's men turn the gun at him. It was not hard to imagine what was probably going through that man's mind as a certain death stared at him. Rumi Khan saw his eyes tighten and then he urged his horse forward.

"*For Samrajya and for Ramaraya!*" the man screamed as the cannon ball tore him in half. His death broke the enemy resolve, and they fled in all directions.

******

Ramaraya received the news of the enemy crossing the river and the defeat of Tirumala's attack. He also learned of Virappa's death.

"Bisalappa, ready the Rachebidas. We will ride in an hour. I wish to be with my brothers as soon as possible."

"Prabhu, the reinforcements?" Bisalappa asked. It was probably the first time he had ever questioned Ramaraya. They both were surprised.

"They will have to pick up the pieces of the enemy that we leave them," Ramaraya told him.

"That we will, Odeya. Hussain Shah will pay for the life of every Samrajya soldier."

"He will," Ramaraya nodded, but at the same time, a single thought ran in his head prominently.

I should not have forgiven him the last time we met.

******

# CHAPTER 10
# 1558

"Hussain Nizam Shah is not stopping, is he?" Venkatadri sighed watching the backs of the fleeing riders.

"Very brave of him, especially after literally forcing us to fight him a needless battle," Keladi Sankanna Nayaka complained.

"Why is he running? I don't think Anna wants to kill him," Venkatadri grumbled.

"Whatever his reason is, Prabhu, he has led us on a wild goose chase for the past three weeks," Sankanna growled.

"Prabhu, a small group has separated from the main force," a soldier pointed excitedly.

"Another rear guard?" Sankanna asked surprised.

"It would have been easier if he had simply sent all his soldiers for us to slaughter in one go instead of sending them at us piecemeal like this," Venkatadri retorted as roughly fifty riders turned and rode towards his men. Their grim faces told Venkatadri that they had prepared themselves for the coming fight that would most certainly claim their lives.

Does he hold so little regard for his own soldiers? Venkatadri wondered at the senseless violence that was about to occur in a few moments.

"Senapathi, shall we respond to their invitation?" Sankanna

asked, a feral grin on his face. He looked exactly like his father, Keladi Sadashiva Nayaka with the same large and powerful build matched with a penchant for warfare.

"Go, try to see if anyone among them has a sense to surrender," he said. At his command, Sankanna led the Samrajya cavalrymen in a charge. The Shahi cavalrymen were better armed than Venkatadri's riders. But they numbered fifty riders, while Sankanna led three hundred Samrajya riders against them. The two lines crashed into each other, throwing men and horses to the ground. The Shahi riders tried to break through and come back for another pass, but Sankanna was an old hand in this kind of fight. Just as his father had done in the battle of Ahmednagar three weeks ago, Sankanna had made sure his men had attacked in two waves, and as the Shahi managed to ride through the initial group, the second group of Samrajya cavalrymen stuck them. It was over rather swiftly. Venkatadri did not give any more attention to the fight. Instead, he saw Hussain Nizam Shah and his remaining soldiers flee across the border and ride towards a large border fort that belonged to the Gujarat Sultanate, his nominal allies.

"What now, Prabhu?" asked a Nayaka officer.

"Nothing, we return and tell Anna that Hussain Nizam Shah has escaped us," he said. "Signal the men to withdraw."

******

He reached Ahmednagar ten days later and found not much had changed. The combined allied army was still camped outside the fortification, far away from the cannons in the wall. The enemy flags still flew proudly over the walls.

"Now what?" he wondered as he rode through the camp. His arrival was clearly expected as his nephew Raghunatha was waiting with two men.

"Uncle was it a good hunt?" he asked, a boyish smile on his face. Venkatadri got down from his horse and embraced him tightly. Raghunatha had inherited the easy likability from his father Tirumala, but the most endearing quality about him for Venkatadri was his dedication towards Samrajya. He reminded Venkatadri of himself before he decided to accept the role as the Senapathi of all Samrajya. He gave a silent sigh as he parted from his nephew.

"How are things here?"

"Not good, we are still sitting outside the fort."

"Why?"

"The commander of the fort, Jahangir Khan, has refused to surrender the fort."

"Why?"

"He says he does not have his Sultan's orders."

Venkatadri gave a frustrated growl, "Of all the idiots..." he took a second to compose himself. "Where is Anna?" he asked.

"He is watching the deployment of assault troops."

"We are assaulting the fort?" Venkatadri asked shocked.

"Peddananna is furious," Raghunatha said by the way of an explanation.

Venkatadri nodded as he walked to where he hoped to find his brother. The camp was massive, housing almost one lakh fighting men and animals. And the servants he guessed were easily four times that number. So, it took him a while to find his brother. He found a large gathering of senior nobles, both Samrajya and Shahi. He made his way through them, many bowing at him respectfully. Venkatadri found his brother seated upon his open topped palanquin. He held a beeda in his hand, his brows furrowed in thought, as though he was alone and not in the middle of a battlefield. As Venkatadri neared, his brother's bodyguard, Bisalappa bent down and whispered in his ears.

Ramaraya turned his head, his face lit into a welcoming smile at the sight of Venkatadri. He was dressed in an embroidered silk shirt, with a purple kulavi on his head. His brother was now in his late seventies, but carried himself like a man a decade younger. He rose from his seat to embrace Venkatadri. If not for the almost two-decade age gap, the two of them could be considered twins sharing the tall and heavy frame with wide shoulders, but Ramaraya now was much more emaciated on account of his advanced age.

"Took your time," Ramaraya said softly.

"He got away, Anna. I did not think it was wise to chase him into the territory of Gujarat Sultanate."

"You did well, my brother," Ramaraya said simply.

"But without him, we don't know how long this siege will last, Abba Huzoor."

Venkatadri flinched at those words, spoken by a man who Venkatadri suspected did not actually mean it. Ramaraya however turned and shrugged.

"We will find a way," he said coolly. Ali Adil Shah, the Sultan of Bijapur and the man who had just addressed his brother as father smiled back, but Venkatadri noticed his smile never seemed to reach his eyes. He still did not understand why Ramaraya called the man a son. Venkatadri knew how it had happened. Ali Adil Shah had ascended the throne at the age of sixteen a few years ago and within a week after the day of his ascension, his kingdom was invaded by Ahmednagar and Golconda. Forced to flee his kingdom in the dead of the night, Adil Shah had arrived to obtain aid from Ramaraya. Blessed with keen wit and good looks, he had managed to impress his brother, especially as his arrival had been a mere month after the death of his young son. Ali had lost a father and Ramaraya a son. The two had bonded in their collective grief. Ali Adil Shah had gained a powerful ally in Ramaraya, who threw out the invaders from Ali's kingdom. The latest war was also triggered by Hussain Nizam Shah's senseless invasion into Adil Shahi kingdom. Still Venkatadri did not trust the man.

"Prabhu, at your command, I will lead the assault," Sadashiva Nayaka said approaching the palanquin.

"No," Venkatadri said before his brother could respond. "A full-scale attack on the fort will be costly and pointless. We cannot afford to lose so many of our soldiers."

"But neither can we sit here for long, Venkatadri," Ramaraya said irritated.

"Let us try another quick raid. Maybe we might uncover some kind of weakness," Sadashiva Nayaka suggested.

"Excellent. I will let you and my brother plan it," Ramaraya commanded.

Venkatadri bowed and walked back to his tent. He felt extremely tired, but knew he had to plan the task well to minimise their losses.

******

"This is a bad idea," Hande Hanumappa said simply, without his usual smile.

*Hopefully Anna realises it as well*, Venkatadri thought. He watched the regiment chosen to make the raid preparing wordlessly for the battle. The men were all volunteers, many of them part time soldiers serving the Nayakas. Venkatadri had insisted on volunteers, he did not wish to expend the royal army soldiers for the task. The men removed most of their armour, dressing in just loin cloths and thin cotton shirts for maximum mobility. One in five carried grappling hooks and ropes. All were armed with swords, but there were also many archers among them who had to cover the infantry during the climb. They knew they would have one chance to overwhelm the defenders on whichever portion of the wall they would assault. Venkatadri deployed the royal army soldiers behind them, in case of a breach.

"Fire the cannons!" he ordered. The combined allied artillery started to pound the walls of the fort. He waited for a few minutes, then nodded at Kishwar Khan. A force of Bijapur cavalry archers rode out and towards the fort. The fortress guns, which had been silent until now, responded but it was very hard to hit the swift riders. Except for a few lucky hits, the riders reached close to the walls in safety. They quickly fired their bows over the walls to force the defenders to take cover.

"*Now!*" Venkatadri roared.

*"Jai Virupaksha!"* screamed the infantrymen and charged towards the portion of the wall where the riders were engaged. The distance from their camp to the wall was some six hundred metres. Less than five minutes in theory, but as he watched, Venkatadri felt a sinking feeling as the defenders first brought forward tower shields to protect their soldiers. Under the cover of the shields, archers started to shoot back at the Bijapur riders bringing down a few of them. The riders quickly reversed, fleeing as fast as they had come before all of them were slaughtered. That left only their infantry who had barely crossed half the distance. The first cannon ball landed killing dozens of men, but the soldiers continued onward. More shells landed among them, killing more men, but somehow a large portion of them managed to reach the walls. The infantrymen threw the hooks while the archers engaged the enemies in an arrow duel. The soldiers tried to clamber up the wall, but it was an impossible task. As they climbed higher, they were hit by enemies who threw javelins, rocks and arrows at them. Many times, the enemies waited till the soldiers were sufficiently high before cutting the rope and sent them screaming to the ground.

The archers were faring no better as the enemy were able to target better from their higher vantage and protected behind the ramparts. The remaining battle was a foregone conclusion. Venkatadri glanced towards his brother, who looked moments from exploding in anger. Only a few soldiers managed to flee back, the dead and dying left below the walls.

*"That bastard! Who does he think he is?"* Ramaraya roared.

"Anna," Venkatadri tried. "We cannot win without an all-out assault. If we do that, we will lose tens of thousands of soldiers."

"We cannot starve them as we would most likely starve before them," Sadashiva Nayaka added.

"I will not let that small fortress commander make me look weak," Ramaraya said angrily.

"Anna, Jahangir Khan does not serve Hussain Nizam Shah, at least not directly. He is here as an ally from Hussain Nizam Shah's father-in-law Darya Imad Shah."

"Are you implying that the man is not even required to be loyal to Hussain Shah."

"He swore an oath to defend the fort, Huzoor, till Hussain Shah tells him otherwise," Mustafa Khan, the commander in chief of Golconda replied.

"Damn his oath, this war should have been over months ago if not for his stubbornness."

"Hussain Nizam Shah declared that he would not surrender till he has a single breath in his body," Ali Adil Shah said with an almost amused tone.

"Considering he plans to flee as soon as we close in on him, I think this is going to be a very long war," Sadashiva Nayaka grumbled.

"Yes, I guess he did consider a certain degree of flexibility in his statement," Ali replied with an open grin.

"I don't care that man is a bully and a coward. Worse, he is also stupid," Ramaraya growled.

"Well, he still is the Sultan of Ahmednagar and without his word, Jahangir Khan will not surrender."

They were thinking of their next move when Mustafa Khan gave a weary cough.

"Yes?" Ramaraya asked sharply.

"Huzoor, there might be a way," Mustafa Khan began.

Ramaraya's eyes narrowed, "What?"

"My Sultan has managed to get in touch with Hussain Nizam Shah—"

"Where is your Sultan?" Ali Adil Shah snapped.

"He is still very sick, Huzoor," Mustafa Khan said instantly. Which was probably a lie as everyone knew, but no one wished to complicate things by reminding everyone that Ibrahim Qutb Shah had only a few months ago been a staunch ally of Hussain Nizam Shah, before changing sides at the insistence of Ramaraya. But he still did not feel entirely happy to fight against his erstwhile ally so had retired claiming sickness.

"If Mahaprabhu Krishnadevaraya was still alive, he would have wiped out everyone just to avoid trying to keep track who was allied to whom at any given moment," Venkatadri thought tiredly.

"So, what is Hussain Nizam Shah offering?"

"He has agreed to surrender the Kalyan fortress."

"That was before all this unnecessary loss of life," Ramaraya snapped.

"If Huzoor wishes to add more conditions, I would be happy to convey it to my Sultan and he to Sultan Hussain Nizam Shah. But I hope you'll be merciful."

"Oh, I have just two trivial conditions," Ramaraya said with a savage smile. Seeing it, Venkatadri's heart sank. He is doing it again, letting his anger rule his judgement, Venkatadri thought. Ramaraya beckoned Mustafa Khan to follow him to his tent. Venkatadri prepared to follow him, but Ramaraya shook his head.

"No brother, I will tell you everything later," he promised, leaving Venkatadri upset.

******

"Anna no," cried Venkatadri horrified, after Ramaraya had listed out his two 'new' terms.

"Which of the two is making you most agitated, brother?" Ramaraya asked calmly as he watched a servant cutting the betelnut.

"Both of them, Anna, but Jahangir Khan deserves honourable treatment. He fought bravely."

"And wasted the lives of seven thousand of our soldiers and at least three thousand of theirs. Did I not give my word that not a stone in Ahmednagar be harmed if he stood down?"

Venkatadri fell silent.

"Why should his life be more valuable than the lives of all those men?"

"Anna, he did his duty."

"Duty to whom? The man who abandoned his country and people at the first defeat he suffered?"

"Jahangir Khan was carrying out his orders from his Sultan, Darya Imad Shah. He was remaining true to his conscience."

"Then let us see if Hussain Nizam Shah will remain true 'to his conscience'. Jahangir Khan's fate rests in his hands," Ramaraya replied, accepting the thambula from the servant's hands.

Venkatadri sighed, "Anna, I agree with you that Jahangir Khan might live if Hussain Shah negotiates with you. But do not treat Hussain Shah like this,"

"Like a vassal, you mean?"

"Yes, he is the ruler of an independent nation."

"The entirety of which is currently under our control. If we take over, divide it among ourselves, there is nothing Hussain Shah can do. I doubt any of his Amirs will be upset, seeing how their Sultan left them to the mercy of his enemies and saved his own life. He should be thankful that I am even giving back his lands."

"Anna if you do this, you will create a lifelong enemy. Hussain Shah might be a coward and a bully, but he is also vain and vindictive. He will not think it as a mercy, but as a challenge. It would be better if you simply kill him."

"I gave my word that he will not be harmed, Venkatadri. I will not break it."

Venkatadri felt frustrated, "Anna, will you never listen to me? Not even once?"

Ramaraya's eyes narrowed, and he signalled for the servant to leave.

"Brother, why are you so angry? This is victory for us. With the defeat of Hussain Shah, we have weakened the Shahis further. Now only Adil Shah and Qutb Shah remain, and both are indebted to us."

"Will you at least stop now?"

"Stop what?"

"You know what I am talking about, Anna. We cannot keep changing our alliances every few years."

"You say as though only we are guilty of it. All of them have changed sides just as frequently as us."

"We must not be driven by their actions."

"True, but neither can we let them stop squabbling among themselves. You know as well as I, what will happen if they stop their infighting. Or have you forgotten?"

"No," Venkatadri agreed.

"You might not have forgotten but let me still remind you. The moment they achieve some semblance of peace, they will look for a new target to unleash their military might on. They must, because it's the only reason all those foreigners keep pouring into their kingdoms. They are in search of wealth and lands for themselves. They will turn their attention to us, raid our border towns and villages, and massacre our people. They have done this from the time Samrajya was established. The history of the Samrajya was one of constant attacks. When we were not invaded, we were raided, almost continuously. I do not wish for that to occur brother, ever again. Not till I am alive."

"When Mahaprabhu Krishnadevaraya..." Venkatadri began.

"Mahaprabhu Krishnadevaraya crushed the Shahis in battle multiple times, even killing Yusuf Adil Shah. Yet, in his twenty-year rule, there were border raids in ten of them. Which increased significantly after they learnt that he was bedridden during his final years. I have ruled as a regent for fifteen years now. There has not been a single border incursion. Every battle that we have fought has been in the Shahi lands. Our people have never been safer in all the history of Samrajya. I have achieved what even Emperor Krishnadevaraya could not achieve. I will not apologise for it, brother."

What could I say that will make him understand that he is taking this too forward. In his efforts to keep them divided, he might end up uniting them instead, Venkatadri thought despairingly.

He was about to reply when they heard a soft voice, requesting entrance.

"Come," Ramaraya said.

Mustafa Khan entered the camp, "Jahangir Khan is dead," he said without preamble.

Venkatadri looked at his brother in shock, only to see a knowing smile on his lips.

"That did not take him much time. Let me guess, he has sent a reply that he has done one of the two tasks, but expects me to waive off the other request?"

Mustafa Khan nodded, "Tell him that had he asked me for Jahangir Khan's life, I would have given that to him. But my demand for him to come in person is not negotiable. His arrogance and stubbornness have cost too many lives for us to count. He must answer for them personally."

Mustafa Khan nodded and left without another word.

"Don't descend to his level, Anna," Venkatadri begged.

"I will descend to any level to keep the Samrajya safe," Ramaraya replied harshly.

******

Venkatadri remembered the days when he was a small boy. He used to hide under blankets in the morning, hoping to give the impression that he was still sleeping. He did that whenever he wanted to avoid an unpleasant morning chore. Today, as the rays of the sun stuck his face through the tent, he wondered if he could try it again.

"Probably not," he groaned as he got up slowly without much enthusiasm. He knew what was in store today and he felt powerless to do something to prevent it.

Damn it Anna, you have already proved your point. Samrajya is already the most powerful nation now south of the Himalayas. A bit of mercy might have been better.

But he knew what his brother would have replied. If Hussain Shah had won, then he would have done much worse to his enemy and thus Ramaraya felt obliged to treat him likewise.

Venkatadri rang the gong near his bed for his servants. They came in and laid out his clothes and brought in food. He took his time getting ready and it was well into the late morning when he made his way to his brother's tent. He found that he was the last one to arrive. At the entrance to the tent, an open space had been created in the night. A raised platform of wood, covered with costly muslin cloth stood in the centre. On the platform sat three thrones, one in the centre was slightly larger than the others. The thrones were unoccupied, but people had lined up on either side of them. Senior officers and nobles of all the allies were represented today. Venkatadri accepted greetings from almost everyone as he walked up to the head of the line. He had barely stood when he heard dozens of drums and trumpets.

Venkatadri's eyes went to the end of the line where a small group of men made their way towards the platform. It wasn't hard for him to identify Hussain Nizam Shah. As he neared, Venkatadri noticed that Hussain Nizam Shah's amour and clothes looked fresh, without any indication of having ridden much.

Strange, did he change before coming for the meeting? he wondered. Hussain Nizam Shah looked at the empty thrones, a murderous look in his eyes.

This is a mistake; this man is like a rattlesnake. Better to kill him now, Venkatadri thought.

"Ali Adil Shah, the Sultan of Bijapur," a servant announced. Ali walked up the platform and gave a stiff smile at Hussain Shah.

"Ibrahim Qutb Shah, the Sultan of Golconda," the servant continued. Ibrahim Qutb Shah held an apologetic look towards Hussain Nizam Shah.

If I had switched sides in the middle of a war, I would be apologetic as well, Venkatadri thought.

"Aravidu Ramaraya, Rakshakarta and Karyakarta of Karnata Samrajya Chakravati, Prauda Pratapa Sadashivaraya."

His brother wore a simple silk shirt with a single pearl necklace. He did not look at Hussain Shah, instead first sat down and greeted the two sultans.

"Let's get this over with," snarled Hussain Shah. His tone made several Samrajya officers glare at him.

Ramaraya looked at him as though he had not spoken, "How was your ride? Was it pleasant?"

Hussain Shah simply glared at him.

Anna do not drag this, Venkatadri prayed.

A servant brought a golden plate with a thambula to Ramaraya. Ramaraya picked it and extended his hand towards Hussain Shah. Venkatadri could see Hussain Shah look at the thambula as if it was a knife and then without a word, he quickly neared it and took the thambula and put it in his mouth. That done, he nodded at a servant who brought him a small pot. Hussain Shah bent as the servant poured the water on his hands, washing his hands. Venkatadri's hands went to his sword involuntarily as did every officer of the Samrajya.

Hussain Shah turned a gleeful smile on his face. He watched Ramaraya struggling with his rage.

"Water," Ramaraya's voice broke the silence, and a servant ran carrying a steel pot. Ramaraya stood and washed his hands silently, his eyes upon Hussain Shah.

Venkatadri went near his brother.

"Anna, he cannot get away with insulting you like this."

Ali Adil Shah was also present by Ramaraya's side. "Kill him, Abba Huzoor. He has misused your benevolence. He knew your hands are tied behind your vow, explaining his sudden bout of courage that was missing all these days."

"If he was not my guest, I would have cut his hands and hanged them around his neck," Ramaraya said angrily.

"If he was in your place, he would have killed you without a second thought, promise or not," Ali Adil Shah pointed out.

"Then let that be the difference between us. I don't need to hide behind my enemy's shield to strike," Ramaraya said. He watched the still grinning Hussain Shah.

"Leave and do not come before me again."

"You will regret this day, I—"

"No more empty threats. Leave, I will not break my promise, but if you continue, I cannot guarantee the actions of my men," Ramaraya said harshly.

Hussain Shah turned and left. Venkatadri looked at his brother, almost pleading.

"No, brother," he said simply and left for his tent.

This is a mistake, Venkatadri thought repeatedly.

******

# CHAPTER 11
# 1565

Ali had hoped for a few days of peace for him and his men, so he had not taken part in the 'pursuit' of the fleeing enemies. Besides Hussain Shah had volunteered almost his entire cavalry for the task and Ali felt their numbers were more than adequate for the task. He wondered what Ramaraya would do now.

"Hopefully, he will garrison Vijayanagara, giving us free run of capturing all his northern territories. That should be enough to weaken him significantly. Probably enough to encourage some of the Nayakas to rebel. That will leave Samrajya weakened significantly," Ali mused.

Kishwar Khan rushed into his tent without asking for permission, his face grim.

"What happened?" Ali asked.

"Huzoor, Venkatadri is here with a large army."

"Tirumala's forces?"

"They are regrouping, Huzoor, under the protection offered by Venkatadri's forces."

"How many men does Venkatadri command?"

"Almost the same numbers as Tirumala. A bit more cavalry."

"So Ramaraya anticipated that his brother might not be able to hold us," Ali thought annoyed.

"What do we do now, Huzoor?"

"Hussain Shah's pursuing force?"

"Has returned."

"Good, then I guess it is time for a war council."

******

Venkatadri stood outside his tent as he waited for his brother. Tirumala rode into the camp accompanied by Raghunatha and his bodyguards. He was smiling but Venkatadri could see his brother carried injuries. He waited as the bodyguards helped Tirumala down from his horse. Raghunatha on the other hand got down himself, his eyes blazing. He too appeared to have an injured arm. Tirumala took a step towards Venkatadri and Venkatadri closed the distance hugging his brother.

"Take me to your tent, brother," Tirumala whispered.

Venkatadri turned, placing his brother's arm on his shoulder for support. He led them inside the tent. Once inside, Tirumala sat on Venkatadri's seat. Raghunatha grabbed the wine jar in the corner and poured wine into glasses. He handed one to his father and another to Venkatadri.

"What happened, Anna?" Venkatadri asked gently.

Tirumala looked at him, tears streaming down his cheeks.

"I have failed Samrajya and my brother, Venkata," he said choking on each word.

Venkatadri looked at Raghunatha who had gulped down his first drink and was now pouring himself another.

"Raghunatha!"

"They tricked us, uncle, sending their light cavalry across the river and then capturing one of the forts. Before we knew, they crossed a significant force."

"We tried to drive them back, but..." Tirumala added bitterly.

"The cannons tore through our cavalry."

"Why did you charge them?" Venkatadri demanded.

"Virappa, the Rachebida commander convinced us that he and his men would clear the way. We managed to destroy significant enemy force, but when the cannons opened, they killed a great deal of our forces."

"You should not have attacked," Venkatadri told them.

"What would you have done, uncle?" Raghunatha asked.

"I would have withdrawn to the nearest fort," Venkatadri replied truthfully.

"It should have been you here, brother," Tirumala said sadly.

"Anna, you and Raghunatha held them off for more than a month. No one expected you to be able to accomplish the feat."

That calmed both significantly.

"The Nayakas from the interior?" Raghunatha asked with a hopeful expression.

Venkatadri shook his head.

"What do we do now?" Tirumala asked.

"Your soldiers? What are you doing to regroup them?"

"We lost heavily, uncle, but thankfully we managed to withdraw in relatively good order so managed to preserve a large portion of our forces."

"You haven't answered my question," Tirumala asked.

"I..."

"Mahaprabhu, Bisalappa, Sarvadhikari's bodyguard asks for Senapathi's audience," his doorkeeper announced.

"Bisalappa?" Venkatadri said shocked. "Send him in," he commanded.

Bisalappa was dressed in full battle armour. He bowed respectfully to Venkatadri and Tirumala.

"Bisalappa, what brings you here?" Venkatadri asked, although in his heart he already knew the answer.

"Sarvadhikari Ramaraya asks his brothers to hold your position here."

"Here? Why?" Raghunatha asked puzzled.

"So, he may join his brothers in their glorious victory over the invading Shahis."

Why, Anna? Why don't you ever listen to me? Venkatadri thought despairingly.

He looked at Tirumala, "I guess our elder brother has made the decision for us," he said trying hard to hide his emotion. "Let us plan the battle ahead."

******

Ali found the war council in a state of well, 'war'. Hussain Nizam Shah and Ibrahim Qutb Shah were standing barely inches from each other, their faces red with anger and exertion. They did not even notice Ali's entrance.

"In case I missed something, I thought our enemies are camped some fifty kilometres south from here," Ali announced loudly.

The two men turned towards him, and Ali got an impression they were expecting him to solve their disagreement.

"Well?" Ali asked.

"Hussain Shah considers us as weak and ineffectual compared to his own troops," Ibrahim growled.

"Those were not my words," Hussain Shah said stiffly.

"Nevertheless, that is pretty much what you wish to imply by demanding that your men would be in the centre of the battle."

"No, what I meant was considering Ramaraya would command the enemy centre, the Nizam Shahi warriors can avenge the dishonour."

"Ramaraya is here?" Ali asked shocked.

"Oh yes, my spies reported that Ramaraya and his bodyguards have departed to join his brother," Hussain Shah said exultantly.

"Ramaraya has ridden from Vijayanagara without the armies from the interior?"

"I guess he decided that they might arrive too late to make a difference."

Ali was stunned on hearing it as his mind caught up to the implications of Ramaraya's decision.

"We can defeat Ramaraya personally, not just his army. That will destroy his power in the eyes of all the feudatories, and Samrajya will fall into a civil war," Ali thought pleased.

"The soldiers of Golconda will not give up the position in the centre," Ibrahim repeated.

"Enough," Ali said angrily. "We have been provided with a golden opportunity to defeat Ramaraya once and for all, and it would need all of us working together to achieve it."

"Then you are happy to let forces of Ahmednagar man the centre?" Ibrahim demanded.

"I am willing to do anything to achieve victory. If that requires Bijapur to give up the position of honour in the centre, then I will gladly do it," Ali declared.

"Then you may do so, but Golconda will not surrender its rights so easily," Ibrahim said unmoved.

Hussain Shah gave Ibrahim a poisonous look, but did not speak.

Ali moved to the centre of the tent, "Do we have the enemy numbers?" he asked.

"Not yet, Huzoor," Kishwar Khan said quickly.

"Tirumala's army?"

"They have mostly regrouped with Venkatadri's army," someone else said. From the corner of his eye, he could see Ibrahim and Hussain looking at him as if flabbergasted by the fact that Ali seemed to be simply ignoring them.

"Oh, I am sorry I assumed that while you two were fighting like children, someone must try to come up with a plan for the coming battle," he said.

"Why complicate things? We know that the kaffir will be in the centre. All we need to do is attack him in the centre with full strength. Once we kill Ramaraya, his army will scatter."

"That's a good plan," Ali said dryly. "Unfortunately, it's also the plan that Ramaraya will be expecting."

"Let him expect it, my men will need less than an hour to finish off the enemy," Hussain Shah declared.

"If words were soldiers, then Ahmednagar would have the greatest army in this world," Ibrahim sneered.

"Why...." Hussain bristled.

"Stop!" Ali commanded. "Let us focus on our common enemy for now," he said with a fake smile. We will get chances to kill each other after the war anyway, he thought drily.

"What if we fail to break the enemy centre?" Kishwar Khan said.

"Are you implying..." Hussain Shah seemed to be preparing to explode.

"He is not implying anything. He is stating a possibility," Ali said bluntly. "We are here planning to fight the greatest battle of our lives. We cannot ignore any possibilities,"

"What do you propose?" Ibrahim asked, ignoring Hussain Shah.

"We must take advantage of the fact that Samrajya does not possess any competent commanders save Ramaraya and his brothers. The path to our victory over Ramaraya is by defeating his brothers on both flanks. That will leave Ramaraya isolated and easy prey to our armies in the centre."

"You want to take one of the flanks?" Ibrahim asked.

"If you lead the other one," Ali replied.

"Then the centre must not attack till we eliminate the enemy forces on both flanks," Ibrahim said looking at Hussain Shah.

"You want me to remain on the defensive for most of the battle?" Hussain Shah demanded, his eyes narrowing.

"Only until we crush the enemy flanks," Ali said soothingly.

"If you cannot follow the plans then let us know, Sultan Hussain Shah. We will not risk our lives and that of our men," Ibrahim said harshly.

"I never said I will not follow the battle plans," Hussain Shah said angrily.

"Then it is settled," Ali announced before the two got into another argument. He left the tent quickly, followed by his men.

******

"Anna, you should not have come," were the first words from Venkatadri's mouth when he met Ramaraya.

"How could I remain behind? When the fate and future of Samrajya is going to be decided here, my brother?" Ramaraya asked. He felt tired, and the long ride reminded him that he was no longer a young man.

Tirumala and his son looked equally tired, but Ramaraya saw both were determined to make amends for their defeat.

"Anna, the enemy have started to bring in all their contingents to battle,"

"What are their strengths?"

"Some fifty thousand cavalry and ten thousand infantry, mainly gunners," Raghunatha replied.

"I have brought more cavalry."

"Where did you get the extra men?" Venkatadri asked surprised.

"I sent an order for every citizen of Samrajya with a horse to join us in this great struggle."

"How many men joined?"

"A few thousand."

"The rest?" Raghunatha asked.

"My Rachebidas and mercenary cavalry of Gilani brothers."

"More untrustworthy 'auxiliaries' and untrained levies," Venkatadri muttered under his breath.

Ramaraya ignored his brother's comments.

"Have you decided on our battle plan?" Ramaraya asked.

He saw Venkatadri and Tirumala nod simultaneously.

"The Shahis will try one of the two tactics: either they will attack the centre, aiming to kill you, our commander, or they might try to destroy our flanks and then focus on our centre."

"Which one of the tactics do you think they will try?"

"We are not sure, Anna," Tirumala replied.

"Have we managed to get some information about the positions of the individual sultans?"

"Yes, our spies have brought that information," Raghunatha confirmed.

"Where is Hussain Shah?" Ramaraya asked.

Tirumala responded, "He will be in the centre, the other..."

Ramaraya raised his hand to stop him.

"Does not matter where the others are, this is what we will do. Venkatadri, you will deploy on the left flank. Under you will be twenty thousand infantry and twenty thousand cavalry. Tirumala, you and your son will deploy on the right with similar forces. You will also have three hundred war elephants. The remaining army will remain in the centre under my command."

"What is our plan?" Venkatadri asked.

"Your job will be to hold the enemy flanks," Ramaraya said looking at both his brothers.

"And you, Anna?"

"I will shatter the enemy centre and kill that bastard Hussain Shah. He is the heart of this invasion; the other Shahis are fighting for glory, he is fighting for revenge against us. If he is killed, the others will retreat."

"Anna, the sultans might have the same idea – of a massive attack in the centre," Venkatadri warned.

"That is why, Tirumala, you will have an important role. You will use your elephants to throw the enemy flank into confusion. The enemy centre will be forced to reinforce the flank."

Both Tirumala and his son's ears perked up at Ramaraya's words, both recognising the opportunity Ramaraya was offering to regain their honour.

"Anna, we will not fail," Tirumala said swiftly.

Ramaraya nodded, "Don't worry my brothers, we will win the battle just like all the battles before," he said confidently.

******

Venkatadri decided to make one final appeal to his brother to withdraw to Vijayanagara, leaving the battle in his hands. When he reached Ramaraya's tent he found his brother Tirumala already outside and waiting.

"Brother," Tirumala greeted him.

"Is he inside?" Venkatadri asked.

"Yes," Tirumala nodded.

"Are you waiting for me?"

"The two of us have a better chance of convincing him versus just me," Tirumala replied.

"Let us hope that is the case," Venkatadri said entering the tent. They found Ramaraya in front of a small idol, praying.

"Sit," Ramaraya commanded, not turning from his worship.

After a few minutes, Ramaraya bowed respectfully and then stood up.

"No," he said simply eyeing both in turn.

"Anna?"

"I will not return to Vijayanagara," he said.

"Anna, don't you trust us?" Tirumala asked.

"With my life."

"Then..."

"I will not withdraw, my brothers."

"Anna, then at least remain at the rear with the cavalry."

"Who will lead the centre?" Ramaraya asked seriously.

"I..." Venkatadri looked at his brother who too appeared to be at a loss of words.

"There is no one who is more capable than me, brother, to lead our armies in the centre," Ramaraya said unmoving.

"Anna, why can't you understand, you are eighty," Tirumala tried.

"Which only means I have the most experience," Ramaraya replied nonplussed.

"You are too old and feeble for the coming battle," Venkatadri snapped harshly. He heard Tirumala take a deep breath in shock at the insult. But Ramaraya appeared to ignore it.

"You are right, but I will still not abandon the battlefield."

"Why not? You are a liability to us on the battlefield," Venkatadri said harshly. He heard Tirumala glare at him now, shocked at the insult. But Ramaraya appeared to ignore it.

"Once again, your assessment is accurate, but I will still not abandon the battlefield. I have lived eighty years on this earth without disgrace. Do you think I would want to be disgraced by cowardice at the end of my life? If there is anyone in this army who fears death, then I give them permission to leave tonight. But I will not abandon Samrajya or its warriors. And I will not abandon my brothers, who are no less than my own sons."

"Anna," Tirumala breathed softly, tears in his eyes. Venkatadri too battled tears as finally they understood what was truly at stake the next day.

Ramaraya extended his hands and both Tirumala and Venkatadri held one hand.

"If I fall..."

"Anna don't..." Venkatadri said angrily.

"If I fall," Ramaraya continued, "Then make sure the emperor will be safe. The empire cannot survive without him."

"We promise, Anna," they said together.

"Then it is time we retire for the night, my brothers, for tomorrow, the future of Samrajya will be decided. Try to get some sleep," he said.

Tirumala stood and left, but Venkatadri remained for some more time.

"Are you going to blame me for my mistakes once more, brother?" Ramaraya asked.

Venkatadri shook his head, "I only wish to spend more time with my brother; it might well be the last opportunity I get."

******

"Huzoor, you must sleep. It's late," Kishwar Khan said.

"In time," Ali said in a heavy voice.

"Huzoor, if there was another way, you would have taken it."

"And that is supposed to justify my actions? I am betraying a man who saved my life and that of my kingdom in alliance with a man who tried to destroy it."

"But do you have a choice?" Kishwar Khan repeated.

"No, I don't," Ali sighed. "All I can do is harden my heart for what I am about to do," he said.

"Huzoor, do you wish to carry a message to Ramaraya before the battle?"

Ali shook his head, "No, Ramaraya understands why I am fighting against him. In fact, he is the only one who truly understands," he laughed.

"But Huzoor, do you intend to remain awake the entire night?"

"No, not much longer," Ali promised. He did not notice Kishwar Khan's departure, his eyes still on the new moon.

It was a new moon night when I arrived in Samrajya asking for aid from Ramaraya, he thought sadly.

******

# CHAPTER 12
# 1565

It felt like just another day to Ramaraya. He sat on his bed, listening to the sound of men and animals preparing for the impending battle. Ramaraya felt a strange anticipation, one he had not felt in a very long time. The last time he had been so excited for a battle was at Diwani, which had gained him recognition of Emperor Krishnadevaraya. And today?

"Today, I will finally gain recognition of the entire Samrajya," he vowed. He stood up and noticed the servants waiting for him.

"Have my brothers already departed?" he asked.

"Prabhu, Mahasenapathi Venkatadri Raya has already departed. Mahamantri Tirumala Raya awaits an audience."

"Since how long?" Ramaraya asked sharply in a loud voice.

The servant quailed at Ramaraya's anger, "Prabhu, he has been waiting for some time. We wanted to wake you, but the Mahamantri forbade us," he begged.

"Send him in," Ramaraya commanded.

A few seconds later, Tirumala and Raghunatha entered the tent, both were dressed for battle.

"Anna," Tirumala touched his feet.

"Vijayi bhava," Ramaraya declared. "Chiranjeevi bhava," he declared when Raghunatha touched his feet.

"So Venkatadri is still upset that I refused to run away from the battle," Ramaraya smiled.

"Anna, he is upset that you are risking your life while he still lives," Tirumala replied.

"I know..." Ramaraya sighed. "Never mind, this battle should not take long. I will speak to Venkatadri after the battle."

"We will win, Peddananna," Raghunatha declared.

"That we will," Ramaraya nodded. "But do not forget your role today. You must hold the enemy on your flank while I attack and crush the enemy in the centre. Our target is Hussain Shah. Once he is defeated, the other Shahis will not stay long," he said confidently.

"We will do as you command, Anna. May Lord Virupaksha protect us," Tirumala cried.

"May Lord Virupaksha and Lord Govinda give us victory," he responded.

"Send for Bisalappa and get my arms and armour," he commanded the servants. He decided it was time for him to go to the battlefield.

******

The enemy deployment was quicker than Ali's estimation.

"That's a lot of enemy soldiers," Kishwar Khan commented. The enemy formed up in the normal Samrajya manner. Infantry forming into a single large block. The shielded spearmen were in front, with archers in the rear. Behind them, in three groups were the cavalry.

"Their cavalry numbers appear to be equal to our own," Ali commented.

"Huzoor, we will be hard pressed to defeat them," Kishwar Khan said worried.

"Who commands the enemy troops on this flank?"

"Venkatadri Raya and Hande Hanumappa Nayaka," Kishwar Khan replied.

"The last two capable commanders that Ramaraya possess. We really lucked out, didn't we?" Ali grinned darkly.

"Huzoor, should we send the cavalry archers?" Kishwar Khan asked.

"No, let's wait for some more time. I want to give Ibrahim and Hussain Shah time to deploy. Especially Ibrahim, as he has the longest distance to cover to reach his position," he said.

"He is not attacking," Hande Hanumappa said, his eyes locked on the enemy, composed mainly of cavalry.

"He is a thinker, Ali Adil Shah. He will not risk an attack unless he feels he can win," Venkatadri said.

"And us?" Hanumappa asked.

"We will see," Venkatadri mused.

"Karyakarta Ramaraya should have deployed our army in the centre by now."

Venkatadri glanced at his friend and noticed the unsaid question in his eyes.

"I did not want to wake him early," he said. An excuse that sounded weak to even his own ears.

"Where do you want me?" Hanumappa asked.

"With the cavalry reserve, you will command two thousand of our best riders."

"Shouldn't that be you, Prabhu?" Hanumappa asked, his eyes raised to his brow.

"I have a feeling that they might be needed on other flanks before long," he said grimly.

"What are your orders for our men?" Hanumappa asked.

Venkatadri saw the eager anticipation in the eyes of his junior commanders, many of whom were his own blood relatives.

"Make sure that the soldiers get enough water, the day might get hotter later," he said. He almost laughed out aloud seeing the disappointed look on the faces of his men.

They are all like me when I fought the first battle, so eager to charge into the enemy, he thought.

"We will not attack?" one of the officers asked.

"No, our command is to hold the enemy in place. We can do that even without fighting," he declared.

"What if the enemy attacks?" another officer demanded.

"Then we make sure they cannot make the same mistake again," he replied with a broad smile.

******

Rumi Khan could see that only half the enemy army had been deployed in front of them and yet even that force was easily double their own numbers.

"How many men do they have?" breathed a gunner near him.

"Quite a lot," Rumi Khan said grimly.

He heard horses approaching.

"Sardar Rumi Khan," Hussain Shah hailed him in a loud voice once he came to stop beside Rumi Khan.

"Huzoor," Rumi Khan bowed.

"Are my guns in position?" he demanded.

"Another ten minutes," Rumi Khan replied.

"Good, once they are in position, you may begin to fire at the enemy."

"Huzoor?" Rumi Khan bowed, trying hard to hide his surprise.

"What? What is the matter?" Hussain Shah demanded.

"Huzoor, I was under the impression the Nizam Shahi army will wait for our allies to deploy completely and engage the enemy forces."

"I promised them that I will not advance my troops against the enemy, and I will uphold that promise. But I will not let my 'allies' get the first blood. That honour and right belongs to me and me alone. That is why I want our guns to start firing at the enemy immediately," he said harshly.

"As you command, Huzoor," Rumi Khan said, seething within. Once again Hussain Shah was gambling away the lives of his men and his allies.

He turned back to his men who had watched the exchange. He glared at them causing many to look away.

"Move that cannon another twenty metres to the left," he roared pointing to a cannon. The gun crew looked at him in confusion.

"Huzoor, the Sultan told them..." one of the Nizam Shahi officers tried to explain in a low voice.

"I am the head of the artillery. The guns and their deployment are my responsibility and I order that gun to be moved another twenty meters to the left!" Rumi Khan roared.

Hearing his tone, the gun crew leapt to obey him. Rumi Khan watched them manhandle the gun into the new position. He cursed his decision to take up the new role under Hussain Shah one final time. The gun was pushed into position.

"Load solid balls into the first line of cannons," he commanded. The first line contained smaller pieces, but they could be fired more rapidly.

"Begin loading the second line once the first line is finished," he commanded.

"And the last line?" asked a gunner.

"Fill them with charge, but not cannonballs," he commanded. The last line contained his most powerful cannons, but they were also the slowest loading ones. Rumi Khan wanted to be certain that their shots would not be wasted. Something in his heart told him that he needed to keep them ready.

"Huzoor, we are ready," he was informed.

Rumi Khan took a moment to pray silently, "Fire!" he commanded. A few seconds later, the first line opened fire simultaneously. The battle had started.

******

The entire enemy front line erupted as tens of enemy cannons fired simultaneously. The sudden violent display of fire and smoke was followed by an unnatural quiet. But Ramaraya knew that the silence wouldn't last for long and a second later, the cannonballs descended on the ground. Most of the shells landed well short of his lines. But one shell landed in front of the infantry, bouncing on the ground and then cutting down dozens of men.

"Odeya," Bisalappa said concerned.

"It's alright, Bisalappa, their shells cannot reach us," Ramaraya said confidently. A few minutes later, once again the enemy lines erupted a fresh salvo. Once again, the shells landed short or missed their targets, but a few managed to land among his men, killing and maiming many.

"Odeya, what should we do?" Bisalappa asked.

Ramaraya observed the enemy lines, which were now almost completely covered in smoke. He tried to locate Hussain Shah, who he knew would be in the rear.

If you are so eager to fight me, Hussain Shah, I will oblige, Ramaraya thought savagely.

"Bisalappa, I..." he barely began when a roar erupted on his right. The sound of thousands of throats screaming in unison. The words clear to Ramaraya's ears.

*"For Samrajya, Jai Virupaksha!"* came the chorus, and that Ramaraya knew meant only one thing.

Ramaraya watched their entire right-wing charge at the enemy, Tirumala and Raghunatha leading from the front on their war elephants.

"Looks like Tirumala has taken upon himself to respond to Hussain Shah," Ramaraya commented.

"What about us, Odeya?" Bisalappa asked.

"Prepare a first wave of twenty thousand levy infantry and five thousand auxiliary cavalry. We will launch an attack as soon as Tirumala makes contact with enemy."

******

Ali had barely finished swearing at Hussain Shah and his rash cannon barrage when he was brought news of Tirumala's attack on their left flank. Worse, he could see a large enemy force preparing to attack Hussain Shah in the centre.

"Kishwar Khan, take two thousand cavalry archers and two thousand heavy cavalry. Ride now to Hussain Shah's aid. I am afraid he will be overwhelmed by the enemy numbers."

"What about here, Huzoor?"

"I will send our remaining cavalry archers to harass Venkatadri, and keep them occupied," he cried. Kishwar Khan did not waste time and rode to gather the troops.

"Take a thousand cavalry archers and harass the enemy," he ordered his commanders. He hurried to carry out Ali's orders. Kishwar Khan and his troops had barely ridden a kilometre when, with a piercing battle cry, the Samrajya forces charged towards the centre.

"Damn," Ali growled as their carefully laid battle plans appeared to unravel in the heat of the battle. But he did not spend too much time upon Hussain Shah's predicament, because only minutes later he heard the din of the enemy war cries in front of him as the whole enemy line charged towards Ali.

Ali mounted his warhorse, *"For Bijapur!"* he cried, raising his sword high and charged at the enemy.

******

Tirumala's ill-timed attack did not come as a surprise to Venkatadri, neither was the deployment of Samrajya forces in the centre in preparation of an assault on Hussain Shah at the centre. But when he saw Ali detach a significant force to aid Hussain Shah, Venkatadri knew that the enemy had given him a golden opportunity and he seized it with both hands.

Venkatadri sent half of his infantry and cavalry at the enemy. He himself followed the main force with another five thousand cavalry and infantry, careful to keep several at a good gap. Hande Hanumappa remained behind with five thousand cavalry and five thousand infantry.

Venkatadri watched the Bijapur army preparing for their own charge. Ali Adil Shah personally led his men on a large grey charger. As he had expected, the two lines collided violently, claiming the lives of many men and horses on both sides. Adil Shah's men rode through the Samrajya lines, preparing to turn around for another charge. But Venkatadri too was an old hand at this type of fighting and as the enemy cleared his lines, Venkatadri and his second line smashed into them,

"Slaughter them, for Samrajya!" Venkatadri roared, leading his men into the fiercest melee.

******

The enemy advanced towards their lines like a tidal wave and Rumi Khan's guns made no impression upon them.

"Huzoor, should we load the third line with cannon balls?"

Rumi Khan shook his head, "It won't be enough," he said grimly, watching the enemy closing upon their lines.

He wondered how Hussain Shah was planning to handle the enemy.

Hussain Shah did the only thing possible; he dispatched a large force against the incoming enemy. But as they charged towards the enemy, Rumi Khan noticed that none of Hussain Shah's elite guards were part of the counterattack. Rather, it was composed mainly of mercenary cavalry and levy infantry. With a sinking feeling Rumi Khan understood what Hussain Shah was planning. So, it did not come as a surprise to him when Hussain Shah came up to him.

"Sardar Rumi Khan, how long before the cannons are ready to fire?" he asked.

"Another ten minutes, Huzoor," he replied. "Huzoor, our target?" Rumi Khan asked weakly even though he already knew the answer.

"*Target? Can't you see the enemy before you?*" Hussain Shah thundered.

"I can also see our soldiers, Huzoor."

"Yes, I know, but sacrifices must be made," Hussain Shah replied in a heavy tone.

Easy when someone else must make it, Rumi Khan thought angrily. But his eyes were upon their soldiers who now engaged the enemy in a fierce melee, unaware of what would soon occur. Rumi

Khan watched his men dab the cannons with water to cool them while Hussain Shah sat on his horse muttering not a few feet away from him.

"How much longer?" Hussain Shah demanded.

Rumi Khan glanced at one of the gunners who gave a quick nod indicating that the guns were sufficiently cool.

"We are ready, Huzoor," Rumi Khan said.

"Then load them and fire! Look the enemy have already broken through!" he screamed pointing at the melee which was dangerously moving closer to them.

"Load the cannons!" Rumi Khan ordered, and his men loaded the first two lines.

"Fire, fire now!" Hussain Shah screamed as dozens of Samrajya cavalry broke through and now charged at the guns.

"Fire!" Hussain Shah screamed.

Rumi Khan raised his hand but hesitated.

"What are you waiting for?" cried Hussain Shah at the top of his voice, moving his horse dangerously close to Rumi Khan.

Rumi Khan struggled to give the order, but knew that if he delayed any further, then his own life would be forfeit. He brought his hand down, but before he could bring it down completely, one the gunners pointed excitedly to the right.

"Huzoor look!" he cried.

Rumi Khan turned and saw in a distance a large force and cavalry bearing the Adil Shahi colours charging towards them. The Adil Shahi commander took only seconds to access the situation before leading his men towards the melee, the cavalry archers cutting down enemy riders as they slammed into the enemy from the side.

"Don't fire," Hussain Shah growled as he took in the battle.

"Mustafa Khan, take a thousand of my Khas I Khel and aid our troops," he commanded.

Rumi Khan gave a sigh of relief as Hussain Shah's elites rode to take part in the battle.

******

Ali blocked a wild spear thrust of a Samrajya footman and kicked the man in the face. He took a few minutes to survey the battle. It did not take him long to conclude they were losing the fight. The strength of his cavalry was in its mounted archery and in the devastating charges of his heavy cavalrymen. Instead, they were being engaged by enemy cavalry aided by enemy infantry in a pitched melee, which did not favour his soldiers.

We must disengage, Ali decided, searching for his banner carrier. He found the man a few feet away, fighting a dismounted cavalryman. His banner carrier had grabbed the spear of one man and was pulling him closer, but a second spearman closed in preparing to thrust him from the side. Ali drew his bow and shot the enemy infantrymen in the back and at the same his banner carrier brought his sword down on his opponent's head. Ali rode up to him.

"Signal the army to withdraw!" he ordered.

"Huzoor," the man nodded raising his battlehorn to his mouth and blowing loudly. A second later, he heard answering horns across the battlefield as his commanders began to rally their men to disengage.

"Follow me!" Ali cried, turning his horse away and riding back towards his line.

******

Venkatadri slashed at his enemy, left shoulder in an overhead swing. He followed it with a thrust at the man's exposed face. The man collapsed from the saddle. Venkatadri looked around for another opponent, but he could hear enemy horns blaring throughout their lines, signalling Ali's intentions of a withdrawal.

"Signal the men to stand fast. Do not chase the enemy. I will personally execute any who does!" he screamed. His order was shouted throughout the battlefield. His nephew, Peda Timma came up to him covered in blood, his eyes wild with excitement.

"Uncle, give me two thousand horsemen and I will chase them off the battlefield," he cried.

If I give you two thousand horsemen, then I will never see them again as the enemy will lead you on a merry chase killing you at leisure, Venkatadri thought. It was a standard Shahi tactic of faking a flight from battlefield and the fact his officers could not seem to recognise it scared Venkatadri.

"No," he shook his head. "We will withdraw to our lines," he said. Barely had he spoke when another officer, his second cousin, another young man in his twenties.

"Prabhu—"

"No," Venkatadri stopped him before he could finish.

"There will be no chase," he said loudly. "Remember our orders. We must hold the enemy here while Karyakarta Ramaraya crushes the enemy in the centre! We must follow orders; we are soldiers not mercenaries," he roared.

He watched them look away in shame.

"Signal a withdrawal," he ordered once more, leading his men back.

******

Ramaraya stood atop his elephant, an encouraging smile on his lips as his men tumbled back into their lines, bloody and battered.

"You have done well. Your bravery has been in the highest tradition of Samrajya," Ramaraya cried loudly. At his signal servants moved to provide the soldiers with food and drinks, while the injured were helped towards the rear where physicians were waiting for them. A shell landed only a few metres from his elephant, covering him with smoke, but Ramaraya did not budge. He saw many soldiers looking at him in awe. He knew how important it was to maintain the morale of his men, so he continued to smile at them nonchalantly.

"Do not be disheartened, this is only a minor setback. Our soldiers on both flanks have won great victories," he screamed, causing the soldiers to cheer wildly.

"We are done. Take some rest and we will attack the enemy again," he continued. That brought more cheers, but not as much as he had hoped.

They are concerned for the losses, he knew. Frontal attacks always tended to be messy, but Ramaraya did not possess enough senior commanders to try anything more complicated.

You were right, brother, Ramaraya thought remembering Venkatadri's constant complaints on the matter. He felt tired as the effort of managing the large army all by himself appeared to be taking a toll.

I will have to rest for a while, he decided unhappily.

"Odeya, the messengers are ready to carry your command to both the flanks," Bisalappa said.

Ramaraya's eyes fell on the two small set of riders. They were regular Samrajya cavalrymen. He shook his head.

"No, send my Rachebidas," he commanded.

Bisalappa seemed to want to argue which made Ramaraya surprised. "You disagree?"

"Odeya, we have less than thousand men around you. Our men have been scattered far and wide, leading individual units and giving support to other subordinate commanders."

Ramaraya nodded, aware that he was using his elite troopers to the task they were not trained. But he was helpless. The Rachebidas were the best troops he possessed, or rather as he was discovering, the only men who could be relied upon to follow his orders properly and ensure the remaining soldiers did as well.

"My brothers, especially Tirumala, must understand the importance of my commands," he said as an explanation. His concern with Tirumala's behaviour was increasing. Not only had he and his son launched an unplanned attack, but he was receiving messages that they had followed the fleeing troops of Ibrahim Qutb Shah.

Hope they haven't gone too far, he thought worried.

******

The news that both their flanks had collapsed arrived almost simultaneously. That caused panic to spread among their troops. Rumi Khan turned his head towards Hussain Shah, wondering how he would react. Hussain Shah took the news rather stoically, then he called for his servants.

"Set up my tent and the royal emblem here," he pointed to a location not further away from Rumi Khan's final line of cannons.

It was a powerful statement. Hussain Shah was basically staking his honour by setting up his tent in the middle of the battlefield. Its capture would be the greatest dishonour to Ahmednagar kingdom. Or so Hussain Shah probably wanted to portray to his men.

It would have been a powerful message, if you hadn't already lost the same to Samrajya forces when your capital was captured and you fled, leaving behind even your family members to the mercy of Ramaraya, Rumi Khan thought. Besides, Hussain Shah was still mounted on his warhorse and had positioned himself and his elite at the rear, away from the tent itself.

"Kind of makes the whole demonstration useless when the men can see that you can flee easily," Rumi Khan wanted to point out. But it was useless. Such subtleties would be lost on Hussain Shah.

"I will not flee the battlefield and I will personally slaughter anyone who tries," Hussain Shah announced.

"Now that might be a better message," Rumi Khan thought as the men considered Hussain Shah's words. Knowing that Hussain Shah was capable of actually doing it meant they understood that they had a better chance against the enemy.

"Is he always so inspiring?" Kishwar Khan asked in a low voice. Rumi Khan grinned at the Adil Shahi officer who had saved their lives only hours ago. They had in that short time become very well acquainted.

"Well, our Sultan is a charmer," he said drily.

"Then I hope he can charm the enemy soldiers as well. Because it won't be long before they launch a second attack."

"A much larger one," Rumi Khan agreed. Considering they had barely survived the previous one, he was not too hopeful of their chances of survival.

"Death at the hands of enemy or death at the hands of my employer. Looks like I really shouldn't have left my homeland," he cursed himself again.

"No, I will not die like this," he promised himself as he tried to come up with a plan that might save their lives.

******

# CHAPTER 13
# 1565

Venkatadri returned to his lines and found Hande Hanumappa with a dozen Rachebidas. Hanumappa was reading something. But he looked up as Venkatadri approached them,

"What is it?" Venkatadri asked.

"The Karyakarta has commanded us to hold our position despite enemy provocation," he said.

"Isn't that what we are doing?" Venkatadri growled but his eyes narrowed as he considered why his brother might have sent the message.

"What news of my brother Tirumala?" he asked carefully.

"Prabhu, Mahamantri Tirumala and his son Raghunatha have valiantly driven off the forces of Ibrahim Qutb Shah and Ali Barid Shah."

"And?"

"I don't understand, Prabhu."

"Have they returned to their lines?"

"Not when I left to deliver the message," the messenger confessed.

Venkatadri gave a silent cry of frustration. His brother had done the very thing he was afraid of.

"Tell my brother that I will maintain my position," he told the Rachebida.

"Hanumappa, you might have to ride to our right flank," he said once the riders had ridden away.

"Why? What are you afraid of?" Hanumappa asked.

"If my brother receives the messages on time, then there is hope. But I am concerned that he is already deep in enemy lines. You might have to go there to extricate him."

"It will take me at least a few hours," Hanumappa warned.

"I know. You better leave now, take five thousand riders with you."

"Won't that weaken the flank?"

"I have enough to hold Ali Adil Shah here," Venkatadri said confidently.

******

Venkatadri had infuriatingly withdrawn his forces back to his lines. Ali's plan to lead the enemy away to a more favourable killing ground had failed.

"What now?" he mused as his men grabbed quick drink and rearmed themselves. Their battle plan was coming apart. On both flanks their attempts at breaking the Samrajya line had failed. Although by chasing Ibrahim Shah, Tirumala and his son had created an opportunity and he prayed that Ibrahim could seize it. But it was not guaranteed, and Ali knew that their position now was precarious. In the centre, Hussain Shah's men had managed to repulse the first attack, but only barely and due to Kishwar Khan's timely arrival. He did not know if they could last a second attack.

"I have to break Venkatadri," Ali thought angrily.

"Huzoor, one of our scouts wants to speak to you," said Inayatullah, his senior commander in absence of Kishwar Khan.

"What is it?" Ali asked the scout.

"Huzoor, a large body of enemy cavalry, at least five thousand strong have detached from the enemy opposing us and are riding east."

"Where do you think they are going?" Inayatullah asked intrigued.

Ali considered it for a few seconds before grinning, "Venkatadri must have concluded that his brother might need help to extricate from his combat with Ibrahim Shah. That is why he has dispatched a force to help them. I bet the commander of the force is Hanumappa Nayaka."

"Huzoor, we should send a messenger to Ibrahim Shah," Inayatullah said.

"Do it," Ali agreed. But he was also aware that by sending Hanumappa, Venkatadri had probably made a serious mistake, the question was how Ali was going to take advantage of it. After a a few moments, he cracked a happy smile as a plan occurred to him.

"Inayatullah, I think I have a way to break this deadlock. This is what I want you to do..." he began outlining his plan to his commanders.

******

Ramaraya was selecting commanders for the second assault when Bisalappa entered the tent, his face grim.

"What happened?" Ramaraya asked sharply.

"Odeya, we have received bad news."

"What?"

"Odeya, your brother, the Mahamantri Tirumala Raya, has been badly injured."

"Will he—" Ramaraya hesitated to ask further.

"He has lost an eye, Odeya."

"Then we must send aid to Raghunatha," Ramaraya said quickly but once again saw Bisalappa's hesitation.

"What?"

"Odeya, Raghunatha Raya..."

"Is he injured as well?" Ramaraya demanded.

Bisalappa shook his head sadly and Ramaraya understood what he was trying to say.

"How did this happen?" he demanded.

"They had routed Ibrahim Shah's forces and decided to drive the enemy from the battlefield. Kumara Raghunatha, led the cavalry after the enemy while Tirumala Raya positioned on his elephant followed at a slower pace."

Ramaraya grimaced as he knew what would follow.

"The enemy led our cavalry far and when they were isolated from the infantry, attacked them. Raghunatha was supposed to have been killed by an enemy arrow. Tirumala saw his son fall and managed to bring his elephant to his aid. The enemy focussed upon him and succeeded in injuring him. His bodyguards managed to rescue Tirumala Raya and Raghunatha's body."

"Do you mean to say our right flank has collapsed?"

"No Odeya, they still hold, only barely. Hande Hanumappa Nayaka has taken charge, sent by Mahasenapathi Venkatadri Raya."

Thank you, brother, Ramaraya whispered pleased at Venkatadri's initiative.

"Their loss is a severe one, but we must not lose heart," Ramaraya declared. Once again, he saw Bisalappa looking as though he wanted to say something.

"What is it?"

"Odeya, the army know of Raghunatha's fall. Many of the soldiers on the right flank have fled. Including the Gilani brothers. The army is in panic and my Rachebidas are trying hard to control them."

Ramaraya swore softly at the treachery of the mercenaries, another thing Venkatadri had correctly predicted. But there was little use dwelling upon it now. Ramaraya stood up and walked outside, he lifted his tent flap and found a great many soldiers standing in small groups talking in silent tones, the fear written clearly on their faces.

"Soldiers of Samrajya," Ramaraya said loudly, making everyone look at him.

"My brother's fall is a severe loss to Samrajya. But it makes no difference to the outcome of this battle. You saw how weak our enemies are, how you were able break through their lines. Their courage and strength hangs by a thread. We can win if we only try again. Who will join me?" Ramaraya demanded. He could see some of the soldiers still hesitating.

"Bisalappa, bring me my horse," he cried. As the horse was brought, Ramaraya climbed up.

"We are not cowards to be intimidated by this insignificant war. Fight on!" he roared.

The army roared in union.

"Govinda!" Ramaraya screamed drawing his sword.

"Govinda!" came the answering response of his army as the soldiers started forming ranks.

"Govinda!" Ramaraya cried again and his elephant riders moved to the front, ready to lead the charge.

"Govinda!" he brought his sword down.

"For Samrajya," the chant echoed through the lines and his army charged. Towards the enemy lines. Ramaraya riding with them, accompanied by his Rachebidas.

******

The enemy reappeared as Venkatadri had expected. He saw them forming ranks for another assault.

"Peda Timma," he beckoned.

"Uncle?" the boy replied.

"You will remain with five thousand infantry and two thousand cavalry. Maintain the defences here," he commanded. He saw Peda Timma's face fall at the command.

"Peda Timma, don't you understand the importance of your role? This fortified position here is our sanctuary. If we maintain it, the enemy cannot swing and threaten our centre. I am leaving you in charge of the single most important position of our flank."

The boy cheered up hearing it, "I am honoured."

"Do not leave this position, no matter the provocation," Venkatadri warned.

"I won't," the boy promised.

Venkatadri felt a strange unease like he was making a mistake by leaving Peda Timma in charge. But he had no other choice. Without Hanumappa, he had no other commander he could rely upon, and Peda Timma was the only choice.

Venkatadri led his forces only more in staggered lines, cavalry in front, followed by infantry and then finally a mix force that Venkatadri led himself. The enemy attacked with their heavy cavalry in front, supported by their archers. The lines collided violently, the enemy cavalry once again managing to break through his lines. Venkatadri led his reserves to swiftly close the holes. The battle was bloody and once again he felt that his forces were getting the better of the engagement. He looked around for Adil Shah's banner, hoping he could locate him and find a way to neutralise him. But there was no sign of the man.

"Where are you?" Venkatadri wondered as he continued fighting fiercely.

******

They heard the welcome news that Tirumala and his son had fallen, and the enemy right flank was on the verge of collapse. Yet that did not make anyone happy as they heard the battlecries of the enemy which told Rumi Khan the enemy was coming for another charge.

"Prepare the cannons," Rumi Khan ordered, watching the horizon for the enemy. A few minutes later, he saw the first enemy, a line of war elephants picking up pace. They were followed by cavalry and infantry.

"First line fire!" he cried and his first line opened fire. The balls landed among the elephants, but only a few scored hits. The animals continued to pick up pace.

"Second line!" he commanded, and another volley was sent at the enemy. This time there were more hits, but again, it did not slow the charge.

"Load balls into the third line," he commanded. His men loaded the largest of his cannons.

"Fire!" he roared watching as the cannons erupted covering his entire army in smoke. As it cleared, he saw that the bigger cannons had landed among the enemy, killing hundreds, but it was clearly not enough to break the charge.

"Reload," he commanded as his troops got busy cooling the cannons for the next shot. But Rumi Khan could see that he would not have the time as there was a good chance the enemy would reach his guns before he could fire again. He was wracking his head when Hussain Shah rode forward, leading his elephants and cavalry.

"Charge, drive them back!" he screamed flinging his soldiers at the enemy in an effort to slow their attack for Rumi Khan's volley.

But will it be enough, Rumi Khan thought concerned. He doubted the cannons even from a close range had a chance to shatter the enemy. He wondered if he should retreat the battlefield with his men.

"Hussain Shah has not paid us enough to die for him," he thought angrily. His eyes fell on the war elephant where they had mounted all his 'pay' that he got from Hussain Shah.

I think I have a better chance of escaping by dumping those worthless copper coins. Maybe I can throw it at the enemy. That might slow them down, he joked weakly. But the thought made him pause and consider as a desperate plan came to his head.

"You," he commanded one of the gunners. "Take a dozen men and bring the coins on my elephant," he ordered. The man was confused but he did not question further, and instead directed soldiers to carry out Rumi Khan's orders.

"Why the coins, Huzoor?" a gunner asked.

"I think I have found the perfect use for them," he said whistling a happy tune.

******

Ali rode swiftly, leading his force consisting of two thousand light cavalry archers and another three thousand heavy cavalry. They rode in a wide arc, careful to avoid the furious battle that was being fought. The enemy force guarding their camp was strong, but Ali had gambled on the fact that Venkatadri, lacking any capable officers with the departure of Hande Hanumappa, would lead the army himself, leaving a less experienced officer manning the defensive lines.

"Archers!" he commanded. His cavalry archers rode swiftly, taking special care to ensure their horses kicked up a lot of dust as they headed at the enemy. Ali halted his cavalrymen, giving them a brief rest.

"Will they give chase, Huzoor?" asked an officer.

"I am very hopeful," Ali admitted. He heard arrows being launched, followed by screams of the enemy. A huge din was heard as the enemy battlecries erupted. Ali could not see anything as his archers continued to ride up and down in front of the enemy lines, shooting their bows and kicking up dust.

"For Samrajya!" came a roar and Ali's face lit up in a pleased grin.

"Got them," he said softly.

"Ready the charge," he cried as the cavalrymen formed tight circles. He heard his archers riding towards them chased by the enemy. Ali waited for a few more seconds,

"Now," he cried as his entire force charged forward.

"Keep your ranks," Ali heard his captains command the men as they tightened their lines and picked up pace. He hoped that the archers had the presence of mind to break away. He brought his lance down as the dust cleared a little. He could see the riders coming towards them. Samrajya cavalry followed by infantry. He enjoyed seeing the shock on their faces.

"Charge!" he screamed delightedly as his heavy cavalry smashed into the enemy. Ali himself skewering a rider whom he assumed was a commander of the Samrajya force.

******

Venkatadri was certain they were winning, so he decided to withdraw a little to get a better idea of the progress of the fight. He led his bodyguards out of the melee when he noticed a few Rachebida riders at the rear of the fight.

"Messengers?" he wondered. Seeing him they rode up to him.

"What is it?" he asked.

"Prabhu, we bring grave news," the man replied.

"What happened?"

"You brother, Tirumala, has been badly injured and was forced to withdraw from the battle. You nephew has gone to Veera Swarga."

Venkatadri tightened the grip on his reins as Raghunatha's face came to his mind. Tears rolled down his cheek.

"Prabhu, your brother has led the army in an attack to avenge Mahamantri's fall."

"He has gone himself?" Venkatadri demanded horrified.

"There was no one else, Prabhu," one of the Rachebidas said simply. "He commands you to hold..." he stopped as the sound of large number of riders approaching them reached their ears. Venkatadri looked at them and his cold hand clutched his chest as he recognised them as Adil Shahi's heavy cavalry.

"The enemy are coming from our lines," one of his bodyguards whispered in shock.

"What have you done, Peda Timma?" Venkatadri cried as he understood that the flank was lost.

"Prabhu, what should we do?" asked one of his bodyguards.

"Do?" Venkatadri repeated, "I have lost one brother, I will not lose another. This battle is lost, but if I can reach my brother, maybe I can still assist him in some way," he decided. He turned his horse and cast one last look at the men he was abandoning.

"How can I face my ancestors?" he thought bitterly as he rode towards the centre where the fate of Samrajya now hung in balance.

******

A freak cannon shot hit Ramaraya's horse, causing it to collapse and sending Ramaraya to the ground. His fall had not been noticed by his forces who continued their ferocious charge, fighting through the enemy forces. Worse while his own men had not noticed him, the enemy had. Many dismounted horsemen ran towards him, assuming Ramaraya was someone of importance. Ramaraya drew his sword, but he was under no illusion that he could fight off a Bahamani cavalryman at his age. As the enemy neared, Ramaraya heard his horses and saw his Rachebidas rushing towards him from all sides. Bisalappa reached first, jumping down from his horse and hacked the hand of the first enemy soldier who tried to grab Ramaraya. He then put himself between Ramaraya and the on-rushing enemies. His remaining Rachebidas following Bislappa's example dismounted and engaged their enemies on foot. The fight lasted only several minutes, but in the end, the enemy fled, unable to stand up to his Rachebidas. Ramaraya's chest heaved in pride at the valour of his men.

"Get me a horse!" he commanded.

But Bisalappa shook his head, "Odeya, you are injured in the leg, please mount your palanquin for the time being," he suggested. A troop of foot soldiers brought his palanquin and Ramaraya sat upon it, surrounded by Rachebidas. It was like an island of calm in the midst of the battle.

"How is our attack proceeding?" Ramaraya demanded.

"Odeya, we have managed to break through the enemy army who are now fleeing back to their lines."

"Excellent!" Ramaraya exclaimed. "Sound the charge, we will follow them close. That will stop the enemy from firing their guns," Ramaraya said confidently.

"Odeya, Hussain Shah might decide to fire anyway, remember Virappa," Bisalappa warned.

"Not if he wishes to avoid being hacked apart by his own men," Ramaraya said confidently. "No signal our attack, we should be able to reach them unscathed."

"Odeya," Bisalappa nodded, he went out to give the order and soon Ramaraya heard war trumpets signalling for a general advance.

This is it, we are so close, he thought excitedly.

******

Rumi Khan saw Hussain Shah's forces break under the tremendous pressure and the soldiers fleeing towards their lines. Rumi Khan's gunners looked at him, eagerly waiting for his signal to unload their secret weapon. Rumi Khan shared his men's excitement. The enemy were rushing in blindly towards them, spread out and in an unorganised mass, perfect target for his guns. There was only one problem.

"Move, you bastards," one of the gunners swore as their own soldiers ran blindly towards their lines, blocking the line of sight for Rumi Khan's guns. Worse, the enemy seemed to understand it and their officers were urging their men to close the distance between themselves and the fleeing Shahi troops.

Rumi Khan was worried. He had one chance at this. And as things stood if he fired, he would only be hitting his own troops.

"Do you need a hand?" asked a voice to his right. Rumi Khan saw Kishwar Khan getting down from his horse. He looked tired, covered in mud.

"Unless you can make all our soldiers magically move out of the way..."

"I think I can do better," Kishwar Khan replied confidently.

"How?"

Kishwar Khan got back on his horse and stuck his finger in his lip and gave a piercing whistle. He then turned his horse and rode towards the enemy, followed by hundreds of his horsemen.

"What is he doing?" Rumi Khan wondered as the lightly armoured cavalry archers rode at the enemy. At Kishwar Khan's signal, his men started to shoot the enemy, forcing them to halt their charge and respond to Kishwar Khan's cavalry. The enemy cavalry rode forward to engage Kishwar Khan, but he simply avoided them, being faster than them. As Rumi Khan watched in amazement, Kishwar Khan and his cavalry kept the enemy occupied in a running engagement, slowing them down significantly. Another ten minutes and most of their soldiers had managed to reach the lines safely, while enemy still tried to bring down the Kishwar Khan's agile horse archers.

"Load one of the cannons with a solid ball," Rumi Khan told his men.

"Taking out the coins?" asked the gunner.

"Yes, fire it now at the enemy."

"But they are still far away," the man said puzzled.

"I know, hopefully it should be enough of a signal for Kishwar Khan and his men," he replied.

The cannon was fired, and it landed several metres short of the fight. Kishwar Khan looked back as if surprised by the shot; then he understood why Rumi Khan had fired. Kishwar Khan waved his hand and quickly led his men back towards their line, followed by the enemy army. Only this time, Rumi Khan knew he would have a clear shot soon.

"Prepare to fire," he said wiping his sweaty palms on his clothes as his men stood poised for his word.

"This is it," Rumi Khan thought as he waited for the opportunity.

******

Venkatadri reached the centre and saw the Samrajya forces break through the enemy ranks before being delayed by the enemy cavalry.

"Ignore them, don't let them stop you," Venkatadri cried uselessly. But the enemy cavalry archers managed to hold the Samrajya cavalry, while a majority of their troops managed to reach their lines. Venkatadri could see the enemy gunners waiting and realised that they were preparing to fire a point-blank volley at Samrajya troops, now that there was no danger of friendly fire. Venkatadri could see the enemy cavalry archers now fleeing and the Samrajya soldiers following towards the waiting cannons of the enemy.

"Slow down!" he screamed at the top of his voice.

"Sound the command to form ranks and spread out," he ordered. The enemy cannons would kill many men, but if the Samrajya armies attacked in waves, even if the first wave failed, the second had a good chance to succeed as the enemy guns would be empty. It was a tactic that Krishnadevaraya had employed successfully in the battle of Raichur.

"Signal the men now," Venkatadri ordered once again to his bodyguards who blew their trumpets loudly, but the Samrajya forces continued to charge in a frenzied charge in a large unorganised mass.

"Form ranks, form ranks!" Venkatadri screamed at the top of his voice, pushed further and further ahead. The enemy guns were now dangerously close and Venkatadri saw that the last of the enemy cavalry archers had crossed back into their lines.

Damn, he thought as the commander of enemy gunners brought his hand down and immediately the first line of cannons erupted, sending projectiles, which to Venkatadri's horror, cut down thousands of Samrajya soldiers in seconds.

"What are they firing?" he whispered, too shocked to comprehend what was occurring. A second line of guns fired once again, bringing down men and animals in thousands. Something passed inches from his ear, striking his bodyguard. Venkatadri turned and saw the man collapse from his horse, dead. A metallic object sticking out of his forehead.

"Coins? They are firing coins?" Venkatadri said uncomprehending. He turned his head, his eyes fixed on the guns where the gunners were now preparing to light the last and final line of cannons. The largest guns he had seen and in them he finally saw what he had always been afraid about.

In the guns, he saw the end of Samrajya.

The guns erupted one last time and Venkatadri felt something strike his forehead.

Anna, forgive me, he thought desperately. That was the last thought in his mind as he collapsed from his mount.

******

Ramaraya heard the three successive volleys of the enemy cannons, and his heart was gripped by a strange fear.

"What happened? What is going on?" he cried, looking wildly at the Rachebidas. He turned to Bisalappa.

"Bisalappa, tell me what you see?" he commanded his voice strained.

"Odeya," Bisalappa said looking ahead trying to make out what was occurring. Ramaraya sitting on the palanquin could not make out much, but the change in expression upon Bisalappa's face told Ramaraya that everything was lost.

"Odeya," Bisalappa's voice quivered. "Odeya...we..."

"Tell me," Ramaraya said firmly.

"Odeya, the battle is lost," Bisalappa said at last.

Ramaraya sat upon his palanquin stunned, unable to believe it. But if he had any doubt about Bisalappa's assessment, then that sound of wild incoherent shouts of Samrajya soldiers told him that his forces had been routed and the enemy were now slaughtering the fleeing soldiers.

"Hurry, we must get Odeya to safety!" Bisalappa roared as his bodyguards moved to put themselves between Ramaraya and the onrushing enemy soldiers who had a single target.

Ramaraya.

******

# CHAPTER 14
# 1565

"The cowards are running!" cried out Hussain Shah.

They wouldn't be human if they did not, Rumi Khan thought as he took in the carnage before his guns. He estimated at least ten thousand bodies lying in the killing field, the number of injured probably even higher. He could see several men dragging themselves away and knew that many would not survive for long.

"Looks like they are trying to regroup," a soldier pointed in an awed tone.

Rumi looked at where the soldier was pointing and saw a large body of red armoured men trying to stop the fleeing soldiers.

"Rachebidas," Kishwar Khan said coming up to Rumi Khan's side.

"Ramaraya's bodyguards?"

Kishwar Khan nodded, "Which means," he said excitedly.

"My elephant," Rumi Khan cried. Kishwar Khan waited with his men as Rumi Khan got on top of his elephant.

"Ready?" Kishwar Khan asked.

"Let's do it," Rumi Khan declared, ordering the mahout to charge the slowly retreating Rachebidas.

******

Ramaraya cried out in pain as he tried to mount his horse, the injury on his thigh causing him immense pain.

"I cannot," he sighed looking at Bisalappa. Bisalappa gave an understanding nod.

"We will carry Odeya's palanquin away from the battlefield," he said loudly.

"The enemy?"

"They are busy looting our dead."

Ramaraya nodded, "Is our army truly gone?" he asked still unable to believe.

"Odeya, we must retreat," Bisalappa said urgently. As Ramaraya mounted on his palanquin, he saw clearly an enemy war elephant charging towards him, accompanied by a large number of cavalry.

Bisalappa saw them as well. "Form ranks, use spears to stop them," he commanded. Ramaraya watched his Rachebidas wield their spears expecting a cavalry charge, but the enemy cavalry did not charge. Instead, they shot their bows at his men, wheeling away before coming back for another pass.

Step by step, they left the Rachebidas on the ground, dead.

"No, no," Ramaraya felt tears streaming down his cheek as his men sacrificed their lives for him.

"Keep it tight," Bisalappa cried standing beneath Ramaraya's palanquin. His sheer presence held the remaining Rachebidas together. But Ramaraya knew it was only a matter of time, the enemy had reduced his defenders by more than half and were now circling like hyenas round a weakened lion.

The elephant rider cried something, and then riders charged at Rachebidas from all directions.

******

Kishwar Khan's riders should have broken through them easily, but Ramaraya's bodyguards fought on desperately. One of the riders reached Ramaraya's palanquin, but before he could grab the old man, the huge bodyguard underneath it swung his sword, hacking the cavalryman at the shoulder. A second and then a third rider tried and all of them met the same gristly fate. Kishwar Khan pulled his bow and shot his arrow at the giant, the arrow hit him in the chest, but the giant was unfaced. He threw his sword at Kishwar Khan who raised his shield to block it, but the momentum of the sword caused his shield arm to swing back and hit him in the head. Kishwar Khan fell from his horse, stunned.

"Take me to the palanquin," Rumi Khan growled, and his war elephant charged the palanquin. Rumi Khan stood on his howdah and aimed the swivel gun on his elephant, his target the giant who continued to smite anyone who came near the palanquin.

The giant heard the elephant's approach and looked up at Rumi Khan with hate filled eyes.

"May you go to your warrior heavens, valiant one," Rumi Khan mouthed as he lit the fuse.

*****

Bisalappa simply collapsed, his body split in two by the swivel gun shot. Ramaraya watched his oldest servant, his aide and probably his last friend die and knew at that moment – it was all over. The palanquin collapsed to the ground as the servants carrying it fled. Ramaraya managed to stand up, using it for support. The enemy officer on the elephant got down and approached Ramaraya.

"You are my prisoner, Huzoor," he said simply.

"And you are?"

"Rumi Khan, I command Hussain Shah's artillery."

Ramaraya gave a weak nod, "It was a good tactic, using the coins," he said weakly.

"Thank you, Huzoor," Rumi Khan said, handing him a flask of water.

"What now?" Ramaraya asked, handing Rumi Khan the flask back.

"My sultan wishes to speak to you," Rumi Khan replied.

"I bet he does," Ramaraya smiled, a humourless smile lightning up his lips. "Let's go," he said, throwing one final look at the bodies of men who had died for him. "Forgive me my brave warriors, I failed but I will eternally be grateful for your loyalty. Know that my last words were only meant for you, my valiant warriors," he said as tears streaked down his cheeks looking around at the carpet of red armoured bodies. He wiped his face.

"Shall we go, Huzoor?" Rumi Khan asked again.

Ramaraya gave a nod.

******

The ride back to the camp was short and Rumi Khan was certain that Ramaraya was fully aware what lay at the end of their journey. Yet he seemed unafraid and when the elephant came to a halt, Ramaraya got down, standing tall in the enemy camp surrounded by Hussain Shah's warriors.

"This way, Huzoor," Rumi Khan led him towards Hussain Shah's camp. Once again, Rumi Khan was impressed by Ramaraya's courage as the old man waved aside his servant who was trying to wipe blood away from Ramaraya's forehead. It was as though Ramaraya was impatient to get over with it.

Hussain Shah rushed out of his tent, an unmistakable look of triumph on his face.

"Welcome Karyakarta of Samrajya, Aravidu Ramaraya, to my tent," he said in a loud voice, opening the tent entrance for Ramaraya to enter.

Ramaraya walked though into the tent. Rumi Khan followed.

"Well done, you have done superbly, Rumi Khan. You and your men will receive three times your years' pay after the battle," he beamed.

Of great more worthless coins and I can't even use them in my cannons this time, he though miserably. But he gave a respectful bow to Hussain Shah.

Inside the tent, Ramaraya stood with his hands crossed before his chest.

Hussain Shah circled around Ramaraya like a cat around a mouse, except Rumi Khan could see that it was Hussain Shah who seemed to be unnerved by Ramaraya's stoic attitude.

"Do you remember the last time we met? When you forced me to accept a beeda from your hands? Did you forget my vow?"

Ramaraya simply continued to stare without responding.

"How does it feel to have lost everything? Where do you think you went wrong?" he laughed.

Ramaraya simply touched his forehead with his index finger.

Hussain Shah probably had imagined many versions of their meeting, but Rumi Khan could see that what was occurring was probably not one of them. He must have expected Ramaraya to be fearful or defeated; instead, he found Ramaraya indifferent. Hussain Shah's gloating appeared to simply wash away, and he did not like it. Hussain Shah's eyes narrowed in anger and irritation at Ramaraya's behaviour.

"Does your master think he can rob me of my victory by not speaking?" he demanded Ramaraya's servant. The man simply shrugged, "Sultan, I cannot answer for my master but today morning he told me that if he wins, he will have lasting glory. If he dies, then he will have died on the battlefield, an honour worthy of only heroes."

Ramaraya pointed to Hussain Shah and once again touched his forehead with a smirk.

Hussain Shah looked at the servant once again. The servant shook his head saying he did not understand. But Rumi Khan understood.

"You don't deserve the honour of dying on the battlefield," he mouthed in a low tone. Hussain Shah threw a poisonous look in Rumi Khan's direction and then at Ramaraya.

"Bastard, even now you try to show me disrespect," he growled. He was about to launch into another tirade when his minister, Hasan Beg entered the tent. He was another of Hussian Shah's favourite and as such his clothes looked spotless clean even during battle.

"Oh, you have come at the right time, Hasan Beg," Hussain Shah beamed once again, "Look who we have here,"

"Huzoor, what are you doing? Ali Adil Shah and Ibrahim Qutb Shah are riding to our camp. They will reach soon and when they do, you won't be able to take your revenge on this Kaffir."

"Take him out and end his worthless life!" Hussain Shah cried, and soldiers spilled inside. Ramaraya looked unconcerned as hands closed on him.

******

The hands grabbed his arms, and he was dragged out. Two soldiers brought a block of wood and placed only meters away. His life was now only moments away from ending and Ramaraya felt no fear. Instead, the only regret he felt was that he was leaving Samrajya defenceless.

You were right, Mava, he thought thinking of Krishnadevaraya, you were right not to trust me with the future of Samrajya, he accepted.

He felt hands showing him forward and realised that he was now at the wooden block. He felt the pressure on his back as he was forced to kneel, head on the block. Out of the corner of his eye he saw a man lifting his sword high.

Forgive me, Mava, for I have failed, he thought as the sword descended and there was nothing.

******

A head on spike. That is how Ali found Ramaraya when he reached Hussain Shah's camp.

No, no, what have you done, Ali thought upon seeing Ramaraya's vacant eyes looking down at him.

"Take him down," Ali commanded to the soldier who carried him.

The soldier, one of Hussain Shah's 'Gazis' shook his head, "This is the right place for a Kaffir," he declared. Ali did not waste another word; he pulled his sword and hacked the man's head clean off. The pike fell from his hand and Ali caught it before it could fall to the ground. There was stunned silence at Ali's action, but Ali ignored them, instead concentrating on getting the head out of the spear.

"Where is the body?" he asked.

"I have it," Ibrahim replied as he rode up to Ali.

"Good, Kishwar Khan, detach a cavalry force. I want Abba's body taken to Kashi," he said in a tone that brooked no opposition.

Hussain Shah stood watching the exchange with a bored expression. However, he did not interfere. As Ali's attention turned to him, he shrugged.

"Would have been nice to have a head on the pike. Will make it easier to capture Vijayanagara. Or do you think we should end the campaign?" he asked. It was not a question, but a challenge and Ali knew that if he refused, then many of his own men would probably side with Hussain Shah.

"If it's a head that you are after, then pick one from the battlefield. I doubt anyone in Samrajya will recognise it from such a distance," Ibrahim interrupted.

Ali nodded, "We can depart as soon as my men depart with Appa's body," he declared.

"You cannot..." Hussain Shah exploded.

"Marching now without giving our tired soldiers a few days to recover would be a mistake," Ibrahim Qutb Shah added.

Hussain Shah was not convinced but with both Ali and Ibrahim agreeing to the plan, he could not oppose it.

"Very well, we will rest for two days and prepare to march towards Vijayanagara," he announced.

Ali turned his attention back to the head of Ramaraya in his hands, as tears streaked down his cheeks.

"Forgive me for what I did, but I swear I did not intend for your death," he said. He looked at Ibrahim who gave a sad smile, "At least he died on the battlefield," he said.

Ali nodded weakly, yet he knew one thing.

I have betrayed the man who treated me as a son. I paid back his love and affection with death, he thought. And there, standing with the severed head of Ramaraya, Ali finally knew the answer to his question. The price that he paid to see Bijapur ascend was too steep and he would never see a moment of peace in his life.

******

From the minute he had landed on the shores of Canara coast, Rumi Khan had wanted to visit Vijayanagara. Throughout his entire journey, Rumi Khan had heard stories of Vijayanagara – of its beauty and architectural marvel. Now standing within the city, he had to admit he was amazed. His visit to Ahmednagar had been a disappointment.

Compared to the opulence of Istanbul, Hussain Shah's capital appeared to be like a run-down hovel.

But Vijayanagara, it was.

"Magnificent," Rumi Khan whispered, mesmerised at the sight and the sounds of the city. He was glad that they did not have to assault the city as Rumi Khan was loathed to spoil even an inch of the place. As their armies approached the city, they learnt that Tirumala Raya who had survived the battle had fled, taking the royal family and important courtiers with him, leaving the city defenceless. The city's authorities did the only thing they could– negotiated with Sultan Ali Adil Shah to spare their city.

Ali had agreed but on the condition that the people of the city would hand over valuables worth ten lakh varahas to the armies. The city officials had agreed. Rumi Khan had taken the opportunity to explore the city. He went with just two men and set about exploring the city, comparing it with Istanbul.

"Prabhu, would you like to have some coconut water?" a young voice asked in broken Persian. Rumi Khan looked down and found a young boy holding a coconut. He smiled and accepted it and drank it. He groped in his sash and pulled out a silver coin, one of his few valuable coins that he still possessed and handed to the boy. The boy looked back at the shopkeeper who was probably his father. The man looked frightened, and he gave a gentle shake of his head.

The boy withdrew his outstretched hand, his smile remaining,

"Gift," he said.

Rumi Khan sighed, he understood the people of the city were frightened and were making extra efforts to keep the soldiers happy.

"Huzoor, look," one of his men pointed out and Rumi Khan saw smoke rising in the distance.

"That's one of the markets," he said.

"Why is it on fire?" he asked.

Then he heard screams and sounds of violence.

"Gazi Hussain Shah! Gazi Hussain Shah!" the shouts reached Rumi Khan's ears. He understood what was happening. He turned back to the boy and his father and ran up to them.

"Go, run away, save your lives!" he cried.

The man looked at the smoke and violence that seemed to be creeping up towards them.

"Where can we go?" he asked holding his son tightly in a voice filled with despair.

As the sounds of violence now spread all round them, Rumi Khan realised that the looting was now spreading to all parts of the city. The city that had been built with loving care by successive monarchs of Samrajya was now being destroyed in mere hours and he was powerless to stop them.

"What have we done?" Rumi Khan wept bitterly at the destruction that was occurring around him.

******

"How did it start?" Ali roared at Kishwar Khan and his other officers who shrank back at his anger.

"Sultan, Hussain Shah's men..." Mustafa Khan hesitated.

"They were not paid for months, and when they discovered that we have to wait outside the city, they lost control. That triggered our soldiers as well and..."

"Why did Hussain Shah not stop them?"

"Some of our witness say he was the one who told his men to take whatever they wanted from the city by the right of conquest."

"Mustafa Khan, take command of my elite cavalry. Put an end to this looting. Those who refuse are to be executed on the spot," he ordered angrily.

Mustafa Khan hurried out of the tent, leaving only Ali and Kishwar Khan.

“How bad is it?” Ali asked.

“Huzoor?”

“When I heard of the looting, my first impulse was to rush outside and take stock of the situation. But when I approached the entrance, I wondered what I would see? When I came into this city seeking aid, Ramaraya led me throughout the city, showing me various places. How many of them still stand? I feel like a traitor, Kishwar Khan. I have not only killed Ramaraya, but I have also destroyed his memory by desecrating his home.”

“Huzoor, we will bring it under control, do not worry,” Kishwar Khan tried.

“I should have anticipated it,” Ali wrung his hands in impotent rage.

“There was nothing to anticipate, Huzoor. Sultan Hussain Shah had promised to control his men. How could you have expected him to fail?”

“Considering his behaviour throughout the campaign, it shouldn’t have come as a surprise.”

“There is little purpose thinking about this now. Our men will restore order.”

Ali barked a harsh jarring laugh, “Seems like I can justify all my transgressions by assigning blame to others. I wonder if god will see it in such a way?” he asked. Kishwar Khan did not respond but Ali had a feeling that he would be judged for his actions before the end.

******

# CHAPTER 15
# 1565

"Huzoor, are you going to the palace today for the feast?" asked his servant as he helped Rumi Khan remove his riding shoes.

"No," Rumi Khan replied. "I must go to the gunnery. The new cannons that we cast last week need some work."

"The Sultan might get angry if you miss too many of the feasts," his wife Khalida added as she handed him a wet towel to wipe his mud-stained face.

Rumi Khan waited for his servant to leave before replying.

"I doubt he will be in a state to notice who is attending his 'feasts'. After all, from the time we have come back from the destruction of Vijayanagara, we have spent the time only in what I can call an endless feast. I can't remember a day that the Sultan was not drunk."

"He is celebrating his victory over his hated enemy," Khalida repeated the excuse that everyone used whenever someone suggested that the Sultan should show some moderation.

He is drinking and whoring himself to his death, Rumi Khan thought disgusted. "At the rate he is spending money, the kingdom will end up destitute once again."

"But the wealth that we got from Vijayanagara?"

"Is not enough for all the spending that the Sultan is indulging in?"

"I am certain that in a few months he will see reason," Khalida replied. "But you must go to the palace. You have already accumulated a lot of enemies and they will use your absence to poison the Sultan's ears," Khalida said firmly.

Rumi Khan sighed standing up, "You are right, I think I will attend today," he said reluctantly.

"I will lay out your clothes," Khalida said sounding only slightly more excited than him.

******

The palace was strangely quiet. Rumi Khan heard none of the usual sounds of revelry. As he reached the entrance, a soldier blocked his passage.

"What bring you here?" he demanded.

"I am here to meet the Sultan," Rumi Khan replied annoyed at the interference.

"The chief minister has told us to inform everyone who comes here that the Sultan is not meeting anyone."

"Why?" Rumi Khan asked.

"We follow orders, Huzoor, not question them," another soldier replied, although they were looking more and more evasive.

"Can I meet the minister then?" Rumi Khan continued intrigued.

The guards again exchanged looks, "Huzoor, we will take your message to the minister, but you can't meet him today," he said in a firm tone.

"Very well," Rumi Khan accepted their words, at the same time wondering what was going on.

******

He was woken up three days later by royal guards, early in the morning and asked to accompany them to the palace. Rumi Khan was surprised but he dressed quickly and followed the men to the palace. He was led into the palace and to the audience chambers where he was met by Hussain Shah's wazir.

"Huzoor," Rumi Khan bowed respectfully.

"The Sultan is very ill, Rumi Khan," he said simply. A chilling painful scream followed that declaration as if confirming his words.

"What happened?" Rumi Khan asked in a tone that he hoped was sorrowful enough. Although privately he knew what 'ailed' the Sultan.

"The physicians are examining him, but the Sultan thinks that the Kaffir's curse is responsible," the wazir responded seriously.

Rumi Khan knew very well who the 'kaffir' was and for a second, he wondered if it was truly Ramaraya's cruse that was claiming Hussain Shah's life. He had been present that day at the tent and Ramaraya had indicated that Hussain Shah would not have the honour of dying on the battlefield.

"What can we do, Huzoor?" Rumi Khan asked.

"We can only pray, Rumi Khan, but I want to know where your loyalties lie?"

"With the Sultanate and the Shehzada Murtaza," Rumi Khan responded.

"Swear it by the Holy Quran."

"I swear it," Rumi Khan declared.

Another long painful cry echoed through the walls and the servant in the corner raised his hands to his ears to block the moan.

"I pray that the Sultan recovers," Rumi Khan said, but he knew in his heart that Hussain Shah would not.

Maybe finally the thousands of poor souls in Vijayanagara will find some peace now," Rumi Khan hoped as walked outside the palace, his hands on his ears to drown the pitiful screams that seemed to continue unabated.

******

## 1580

"Huzoor, the Canara chiefs have accepted your offer. In return for our aid against the marauding Portuguese, they will agree to pay tributes," Kishwar Khan declared happily, behind him were multiple chests filled with gold and precious metals provided by the Canara chiefs as proof of their loyalty.

"Congratulations, Huzoor," Ikhlas Khan beamed.

"Huzoor, your dream has come true. Bijapur is now the true successor of the Bahmani Sultanate," Kishwar Khan declared.

"My dream," Ali mused amidst the cheering in the hall. "Yes, I did wish to make Bijapur the most powerful sultanate," he accepted. But now when Bijapur had become the most powerful sultanate in the Deccan, he found that it did not bring him happiness. The dark mood that seemed to have become his constant companion after the fateful battle reared its head again. Ali felt suffocated in the hall.

"Uncle, are you alright?" came the small voice on his left. His nephew Ibrahim looked at Ali with concern. The boy at nine years of age was too young to be sitting in the assembly but as Ali's successor, Ali insisted that the boy attend the meeting every day. It would help the boy understand what would be expected of him in the future, and make the nobles get used to the idea that Ibrahim was Ali's successor. The boy was intelligent enough, but Ali felt he was rather sweet-natured, which might be misused by his favourites in the future.

"I will have to spend more time training him personally," he decided. He squeezed the boy's shoulder gently and the boy smiled happily. The rest of the meeting was spent discussing the perennial shortage of wealth that the Sultanate seemed to suffer from, especially when public works were proposed.

"I must do something about it," he decided. Once the meeting was over, he decided to take a walk in his garden.

******

Ali examined the guava tree noting the areas where the rot had set. He glared at the head gardener and the man flinched, "Huzoor, I have asked the rotten portion to be removed. It's a task that requires great skill and the man who can do it has been sick for the past two days. If he does not come tomorrow, then I will remove it personally."

"See that I don't find it again tomorrow," he said harshly. The gardener bowed quickly before fleeing.

Ali sighed continuing his walk. He found he was unable to ease his mind even after spending nearly an hour in the garden. He stopped at the pavilion erected in the centre where many birds and animals roamed freely. A few deer came towards him, hoping to get fruits that Ali often carried to feed them.

"I am sorry, I don't have anything today," he patted the flanks of a deer who walked away slowly in disappointment. Ali sat on a chair inside the pavilion, shading his face from the midday sun.

He closed his eyes as the melancholy mood threatened to take him back to Hussain Shah's tent and finding Ramaraya's head on a pike.

"I should have come sooner," he chided himself like he had done almost daily after returning to Bijapur at the end of the war. Except no amount of self-flagellation seemed to be enough to rid him of the haunting images of Ramaraya's head. As the years passed, Ali had often wondered whether the cause of his bad fortune, especially his lack of an heir was due to divine punishment.

Ali leaned back on his seat, and reached for the hookah that was kept to his right. He placed the pipe in his mouth and pulled deeply, letting the smoke dull his senses. He heard the rustle of leaves and opened his eyes to see two men approaching him. Both had covered their faces with tails of their turbans and carried daggers. Ali got up quickly. The first man slashed at Ali's chest, but Ali jumped back avoiding the blade. Before he could try a second swing, he grabbed his arm and pivoted him in a circle and at his companion who was charging towards them. The two men dashed into each other, knocking the turban off one of them. Ali's eyes widened as he recognised the man. He was one of the eunuch servants of his nephew Ibrahim.

"Ibrahim? Is he trying to kill me? Why?" Ali wondered but realised he had to run away. He turned and had barely taken a few steps when he felt a piercing pain in his back. Ali moved his right hand to the site of pain and found a knife buried inches from his chest. He tried to run, but found he was unable to, due to the blood loss. The two men caught up with him and Ali felt a second piercing pain in his abdomen. He tried to punch the man, but his movements were becoming slow, and the man simply arched his head backward to avoid it.

Ali collapsed to the ground and the two men now looped over him, their knives raised high. As unconsciousness approached him, Ali felt a strange peace settle upon him.

"Looks like my betrayal will not go unanswered," he laughed sadly as the steel blade entered his chest. Then there were no more thoughts.

******

# BIBLIOGRAPHY AND REFERENCES

1. Heras, Father Henry. *The Aravidu Dynasty Of Vijayanagara.* Madras: B.G. Paul & Co Publishers, 1927.
2. Pillai, Manu. *The Rebel Sutans: The Deccan from Khilji to Shibaji.* Delhi: Juggernaut Books, 2018.
3. Sewell, Robert. *A Forgotten Empire: Vijayanagara.* Meerut: Mastermind Publication, 2012.
4. Kamat, Dr. Suryanath U. *Krishnadevaraya Of Vijayanagara And His Times.* Karnataka: IBH Prakashan, 2009.
5. Stein, Burton. *The New Cambridge History of India: Vijayanagara.* Delhi: Cambridge University Press, 2005.
6. Patil, Madhau P. *Court Life Under the Vijayanagara Rulers.* Delhi, BR Publishing Corporation, 1999.
7. Sandhu, Maj Gen Gurcharn Singh. *A Military History of Medieval India.* Delhi: Vision Books, 2003.
8. Eaton, Richard. *A Social History of the Deccan, 1300–1761: Eight Indian Lives.* Delhi: Cambridge University Press, 2005.
9. Heras, Father Henry. *Beginnings of Vijayanagara History.* Bombay: Indian Historical Research Institute, 1929.
10. Salatore, R.A. *Social and political life in the Vijayanagara empire (A.D. 1346-A.D. 1646).*
11. Briggs, John. *History Of The Rise Of The Mahomedan Power In India.* Delhi: Gyan Publishing House, 2021.

12. Shastri, Nilakants. *A History of South India (Oip): From Prehistoric Times to the Fall of Vijayanagar*. Delhi: Oxford University Press, 1997.

13. Dallapiccola, Anna. *The Great Platform at Vijayanagara: Architecture & Sculpture*. Delhi: Manohar Publishers, 2012.

14. Sarma, P Sree Rama. "Rama Raya's Policy". https://www.jstor.org/stable/44138841

15. Shivarudraswamy, S.R. "Hindu-Muslim Relations Under the Vijayanagara Empire". https://www.jstor.org/stable/44145855

16. Wagoner, Phillip B. "Sultan among Hindu Kings": Dress, Titles, and the Islamicization of Hindu Culture at Vijayanagara. https://www.jstor.org/stable/2646526

17. Morrison, Kathleen D. and Carla M. Sinopoli. "Dimensions of Imperial Control the Vijayanagara Capital". https://www.jstor.org/stable/682381

18. Sinopoli, Carla M. "From the Lion Throne: Political and Social Dynamics of the Vijayanagara Empire". https://www.jstor.org/stable/3632447

19. Verghese, Anila. "Deities, Cults and Kings at Vijayanagara". https://www.jstor.org/stable/4128340

20. Naik, H.P. Keshava. "Some Aspects Of Feudalised Segments In The Vijayanagara Polity". https://www.jstor.org/stable/44141248

21. Eaton, Richard. "'Kiss My Foot', Said the King: Firearms, Diplomacy, and the Battle for Raichur, 1520". https://www.jstor.org/stable/20488080

22. Ahmad Khan, Iftikhar. "The Import of Persian Horses In India 13-17th Centuries". https://www.jstor.org/stable/44140214